THE EDUCATION
of a
PSYCHIATRIST

THE EDUCATION

of a

PSYCHIATRIST

*Human Encounters in the
Field of Vulnerability*

SHEILA HARMS

SUNY
PRESS

Cover credit: Eugène Jansson. *Evening Mood-Lidingö*. 1900. Oil on canvas. 35 1/2 x 66 3/8 in. The Cleveland Museum of Art. Mr. and Mrs. William H. Marlatt Fund. 2005.4. https://www.clevelandart.org/art/2005.4

Published by State University of New York Press, Albany
© 2025 State University of New York
All rights reserved
Printed in the United States of America

EU GPSR Authorised Representative:
Logos Europe, 9 rue Nicolas Poussin, 17000, La Rochelle, France
contact@logoseurope.eu

For information, contact State University of New York Press, Albany, NY
www.sunypress.edu

Library of Congress Cataloging-in-Publication Data

Names: Harms, Sheila author
Title: The education of a psychiatrist : human encounters in the field of
  vulnerability / Sheila Harms.
Description: Albany : State University of New York Press, [2025] | Series:
  SUNY series, transforming subjects : psychoanalysis, culture, and
  studies in education | Includes bibliographical references and index. |
  Identifiers: LCCN 2024062270 | ISBN 9798855803570 (hardcover) | ISBN
  9798855803594 (ebook) | ISBN 9798855803587 (paperback)
Subjects: LCSH: Psychiatry—Study and teaching
Classification: LCC RC459.H367 2025 | DDC 616.890076—dc23/eng/20250519
LC record available at https://lccn.loc.gov/2024062270

*This book is dedicated to the memory
of my late parents, Elsie and Jake*

Contents

Acknowledgments

This first thank you is to Rebecca Colesworthy at SUNY Press for her generosity and support in the process that is this book. Thanks to skilled copy editor Catherine Mitro for sharing her understanding of Arendt with me and her thoughtful attention to finding my voice. And then there are the people in my life who created and nurtured the conditions for the making of this manuscript. For introducing me to Dr. Deborah Britzman and being a source of intellectual heft in my life, a sincere thank you to Dr. Susan Giroux. For the most profound privilege of working alongside the truly brilliant mind of Dr. Deborah Britzman, I am forever changed. With all of the gratitude I can convey, thank you, Deborah, for bringing into clarity an emotional logic that was always present for me but not fully known until the joy of encountering you. To Dr. Alice Pitt for her incisive read on everything; I also want to express my sincere gratitude for the ways in which my scholarship has been deeply affected by you. To Dr. Christine Vanderkooy, thank you for a longtime friendship born out of making music that writes its own melody into the work of this manuscript. To my dear friend Dr. Karen Saperson, who has somehow managed to be exactly what I need; you are a mentor, guide, inspiration, and dearest of friends, and have been an emotional container in seeing me through this project with your remarkable skills and deep humanity. Dr. Harriet MacMillan, your belief in the possible and your tenacity to follow it have been written into this text. To Dr. Vic Neufeld and Barbara Neufeld — for the countless dinners on the Chedoke Avenue deck where you spoke in ways that made medicine possible and, subsequently, this book, I am sincerely grateful to you both. For the friendships that survive medical school and go on to embody the stuff of too good to be true, I am more than grateful. Here, I am referring to Dr. Janine Davies and Dr. Sheryl McClaren — thank you for your constancy and immovability that coalesced in the time of learning medicine together and has sustained me since. To Dr. Godfrey Rukundo, my colleague, trustworthy friend, and coconspirator in striving to make education better than it is — thank you for believing that we could build a program with origins a world apart. To the students whose brave curiosity have demanded that I find my own learning stance, precisely when I was resistant to it, thank you. To my patients and their families, who have taught me what it means to be a physician with a heart, your inspirations born of human pain and grit are daily gifts in medical practice. To my Tante Sue, thank you for your interest and constancy in my life. To my sister Carla, thank you for being family and for the steadfastness of you. To my friend and mother-in-law Carol, thank you for your love and confidence in me. And, finally, to Warren; thank you for chopping wood and carrying water while I labored to write. I love you with all my heart.

On Making Psychiatry
an Educational Problem

A psychiatrist is presumed to be expert in their work with individuals whose minds signal a painful departure from certain predictable reaches. At least, this is what I wanted to believe when I started training. The breach of confidence, to my surprise, was deeply felt by both patient and healer alike when I was forced to reflect on crucial problems that materialized when the *know-how* in the custodianship of psychiatric care infrequently translated into *show how.* Even as I listened to my patients as I had been taught to do, and could simultaneously identify and efficiently catalogue symptoms, I soon learned that the promised empirical healing of diagnostics and related treatment algorithms fell short of the healing sought by all of us. In these disorienting clinical encounters, where it was clear that something wasn't right, a pedagogical conundrum emerged for me that only belatedly registered as uncomfortable emotional symptoms about what I thought I had been taught to rely on. My medical education fell short of the confidence it promised.

It strikes me that this tangled nidus of professional confusion and uncertainty not only creates the context for my inquiry into the complexities and dilemmas of contemporary matters of medical education but also reframes psychiatry itself as an educational problem. It may then be reasonably asked, What is an educational problem? From a technical perspective, the health profession's literature offers a description of an educational problem as a type of personal lack. More specifically, individuals are without particular skills, or knowledge, or attitudes that confound the professional's ability to do what they are trying to do (Kitto 2019). Perhaps not surprisingly, this deficiency state does not quite capture the transference dilemmas, otherwise thought of as emotional situations, that seem to take center stage when the human is the subject of scarcity. The human scope of educational problems comes to life when Deborah Britzman (2011) states, "All at once, the force of education expands to unimagined scenes and to what is unimaginable in the self. In any of its guises, education becomes our studio for human nature" (9). As it turns out, much can go wrong in the studio.

In returning to my psychiatrist voice as a way of coming to medicine as an education in a learning profession, I tackle two overarching problems in the following essays. The first problem is personal in nature in that I explore numerous dimensions in thinking about why psychiatry is an educational problem for me. I wear many hats in my experience as a psychiatrist: professional learner, clinician, teacher, supervisor, and reader in the field. In these encounters of psychiatry, I find different conflicts, challenges, vagaries, and vicissitudes that speak educationally to the places where the center will not hold. More on this later. Secondly, I have encountered different vantage points speaking about how those in psychiatry are educated. The second problem is therefore interrogating the path to arriving at a practice of the mind using orientations such as literature, philosophy, social sciences, memoirs, health sciences, and historical texts. Broadly speaking, these two dimensions often find themselves at odds with each other, and in doing so, also speak to each other, opening new ways of thinking for me about how we separate the practitioner from the practice while simultaneously being educated.

While there are many texts that can help support the idea of problematizing psychiatry itself as an educational problem, Jonathan Rosen's (2023) recent memoir, *The Best Minds: A Story of Friendship, Madness, and the Tragedy of Good Intentions*, is a contemporary account of his relationship with a lifetime friend whose psychiatric illness leads to a murderous crime enacted within a devastating paranoid delusion. Yet it is not the fatal blow that makes the story so compelling but rather Rosen's determined efforts to understand his own and other's lives shaped by an illness that eluded people until it was too late. The sheer physicality of his novel dedicates hundreds of pages to a story that struggles to conclude, although the wieldy pagination doubles as another attempt to understand what confounds the mind. Rosen leaves no stone unturned in examining the collision points of mental health law, psychiatry, psychology, deinstitutionalization, pharmacology, culture, literature, and politics only to reach a heart-wrenching cadence acknowledging that a brilliant mind could not save itself. The story performs what many psychiatrists have experienced in treating individuals with schizophrenia: observing the benefits of antipsychotic medications in subduing delusions and hallucinations, being mindful of the sinkhole that constitutes community mental health infrastructure, the dearth of tangible support for patients' families often leaving them at their wit's end in trying to help, cumbersome mental health law, and hearing patients repeatedly say that they do not want to adhere to medications. Devastation ensues despite best efforts.

How then does Rosen's memoir help me situate psychiatry as an educational problem? The revolving door of conflicted challenges that Rosen so thoughtfully captures constitutes the very conditions of the educational problem within psychiatry and problematizes psychiatry as a practice representing the potential for the unthinkable, the unknowable, and the brittleness that confound human capacity. The toggling between the personal and the professional within Rosen's memoir is deeply felt; the endearing spirit of childhood friendship and the potential of bright minds in contrast to the professional betrayal where mental illness cannot be sufficiently corralled through pharmacology, the repetition of dizzying attempts to help, and the love of a dedicated partner. Schizophrenia displaces the ability of a brilliant mind to subvert its own deadly course. Understanding the science behind schizophrenia and the desperate plea for healing are often seen as one and the same. In the end, we do not know how to make Rosen's story of his friend Michael Laudor other than what it becomes. We know the disastrous plot before the page is turned, but we read anyway, hoping for a different outcome and for a reprieve from the anxiety of determined anticipation.

I do not read Rosen's memoir as a warning signal nor as alarmist in nature. Instead, Rosen's writing in the form of his memoir is a fork in the road for me because it echoes of the social sphere of psychiatry and the hopes for social reform within the practice. Rosen's memoir highlights the kinds of intersubjective conversations I am interested in that require an understanding of psychiatry as a historical practice as well as a nexus of practice histories that sets the stage for what it means to undergo an education within the field. In the following essays, I attempt to draw upon the arc of psychiatry's history to situate my own storied education, as well as pay close attention to the experience of others who have engaged an education in the practice of the mind. In thinking about how I am trying to understand my own education, my practice of psychiatry, what came before, and how it all works out in the end, I am led down a reflective path where the quality of interweaving ideas first registers as incoherent but later becomes intelligible by way of a social exchange with applied pedagogical tools such as repetition, imitation, play, and thought harmonization. John Forrester (2017) put words to this aesthetic and described it as rhizomic in its lateral, winding, intertwined application and performance (1) and used this description to introduce what he felt was an underrecognized method of reasoning: thinking in cases. He had long been interested in the history and philosophy of science and its social proclivities. However, it was the historical case, precisely the psychoanalytic case, that gave him cause for serious consideration about the scientific place of the individual within the human sciences.

Relying on Forrester's orientation offered in his framework *thinking-in-cases* would have me ask what it is about critical histories in psychiatry that make them interesting cases, or even exemplars for further educational interrogation? Specifically, I am interested in looking at how psychiatry critiques testimonies from practitioners such as Oliver Sacks and Michel Foucault as well as how psychodynamic orientations to these narratives intertwine to illuminate the dilemmas encountered within psychiatry, their meaning, and applications to an education of an educator in a caring profession. I work with education as an object to be subjectively engaged, and as a condition — particularly of temporality — that signifies a site of affect and historical attachments as well as a spatial void that permits me to come to an educational conclusion that no matter how I work it, things will and have gone wrong. But this is not the end of the story. Rather, it is the beginning.

The essays in this volume understand education through deeply personal queries, which bring me to an unusual but rich interdisciplinary engagement. As I draw from Forrester's (2017) frame of thinking in cases, I consider the work of *climbing inside one's head* when reading the memoir of Sacks (2016), whose work in neurology also grapples with questions of the mind. I also find myself iteratively needing a thought banister and grab on to affiliations with history and philosophy to reconstruct an understanding of my contemporary educational experience in which my gendered self has been removed from my current professional belonging. To engage in such a reconstruction, I rely on Foucault's critiques of psychiatry as a practice plagued by a type of frailty where my own observations about gender in medicine ring true instead of seeming outdated. In linking Foucault's interpretations to Sacks's recall of numerous institutional encounters in medicine, I encounter a psychiatric history predicated on gendered omissions. These omissions lead me to tackle the thorny problem of matricide, envisioning an elimination of an educational mother, and where this dead end can, in fact, be an educational beginning. These intersections wind their way to Uganda, a place where my experiences as a clinician-educator engage a discourse relying on a kind of disassembling and unlearning. These descriptions lead me to the concept of an educational void ruthlessly encountered as a situational dilemma and how I simultaneously underwent a thought transformation to understand it as a survival tactic.

I find affect is a constant theme predictably acting to break open educational encounters with colleagues, patients, memoirs, and those learning a profession of caring. As a result, I lean heavily on psychoanalytic orientations throughout to highlight the emotional logic inherent in the transference sites constituting the human work of medical practice and education. Looking over my educational experiences, major dilemmas emerge: What do bodies, their gender, or sex have to do with a practice of psychiatry, presumably organized by questions of the mind? What does my body have to do with my education? The novelty of my discussion carries the insistence that the body itself can be read as an educational marker and can be used to highlight an experiential pedagogy to make the mind intelligible in its relevance to the temporality of education. I arrive at the fault lines of education where pretending becomes practice, difficult knowledge runs amock, and the uncertainties, including the frailty of my own self as a resource for the mind, often constitute the very educational myths I need to tackle as obstacles to learning. Through this process, a personal and professional awakening occurs.

In the chapter descriptions that follow, the conditions of education are presented through personal autoethnographic reflections as a child and adolescent psychiatrist who had to undergo an education within psychiatry to arrive where I am. My examinations of this experience are written against academic observations provided by a number of scholars who have also struggled with questions of the mind and, in doing so, with what it means to create intelligibility while enduring education. The assumptions that come to bear in this volume are similar to those of psychoanalysis — namely that medical education inherits the incompleteness of the past, that the experiences of the self are always in the middle of something, and that feeling often happens before knowing. The vulnerabilities of working through form a new understanding of what it meant to discover my mind through the experience of losing it, while at the same time having to negotiate a therapeutic, if not curative, psychiatric practice with those who look to me for expertise.

Lines of Inquiry

Chapter 1 introduces early experiences of child psychiatry marked by a curriculum of surprises and failures, setting the stage to explore expectations of how psychiatry should be. Controversial ideas about what constitutes the education of a psychiatrist and what education itself is made of are interrogated in the uncertain space of learning the practice of psychiatry while simultaneously not knowing what to do. Using the technique of free association, readers are led back into the classroom of the psychiatrist, where a constant state of unknowing sets the stage as a condition for learning. Through assessments of risk pertinent to both patient and practitioner, as well as learning what it means to lean on empirical evidence for a false sense of security, an education in psychiatry becomes a dangerous place. Danger is not always immediately identifiable, but the affective pull that is experienced in education as bracing for impact signals something nefarious at play. However, dangerous places are also capable of leading one to generative openings such as the discovery of historical writers like Sacks. Sacks's own personal memoirs act as a compass to guide my thinking and reflections throughout.

Chapter 2 turns to a close reading of Sacks's (2016) memoir of his education, *On the Move: A Life*. He is not a psychiatrist, yet as a neurologist who crosses so many boundaries of genre and fields, he meticulously works with material that would often be found in psychiatry. Sacks takes up questions of the mind, perceptions of pathological thought and behavior, and how these queries relate to himself in a learning profession as well as to his patients. I use Sacks's memoir as a mirror to my educational encounters in psychiatric training. Relying on his firsthand account as a student, I ask when learning begins and when language becomes accessible to describe the events surprisingly salient to learning. I also focus on the place and positioning of the body as an educational marker speaking to a different kind of experiential pedagogy predicated on somatic revelations and its relevance to the temporality of education. Through Sacks, I come to understand that his unexpected learning is always in the time of after, or what Sigmund Freud (2006) refers to as *Nachträglichkeit*, where distress is attached to the memory of the learning event instead of the learning event itself. This kind of anxious waiting condition as a framework for *knowing* in medicine is also explored personally when I speak about perceived professional failures encountered through death and dying in medicine. Finally, my exploratory reading of Sacks focuses on what sex and sexuality has to do with medicine and an education within it, tackling the fragilities of belonging in this learning environment.

Chapter 3 leans on the work of Foucault in his lectures *Psychiatric Power* (2006), and I take up questions of the body in psychiatry through embodied conflicts rendered palatable by authoritative forces. Specifically, this chapter is guided by three questions: What does the body have to do with a practice of healing the mind? What kind of bodies have constituted the historical work of psychiatry? How might these observations map onto gendered conceptualizations of my own education and contemporary practice in psychiatry? Weaving in and out of historical observations made by Foucault about psychiatry and linking them to Sacks (2016) and his numerous medical institutional encounters recalled as memoirs, I explore the problem of my own emergence in the history of academic psychiatry, leading me to introduce the idea of educational matricide in an arena weary of educational newness. This perilous curriculum also shows itself to be paradoxically generative in its intent.

Chapter 4 relies on Sacks's (2016) experience with *hospital people* — those who are viewed as an effect of the challenges associated with the medical establishment — and how he navigated these spaces and often hostile relationships. I include critical histories in psychiatry, such as the work of Foucault in his lectures *Psychiatric Power* (2006), where his historical observations of the asylum ring truer in contemporary psychiatry than is comfortable to admit. Foucault writes about the subversive and regime-like power dynamics found in psychiatric institutions embedded within a controversial history intended to control madness through a subjectifying, disciplinary apparatus, also simultaneously viewed as a practice of psychiatry. I read Sacks's relational use of his own body and how it differs from historical accounts as an exemplar in probing questions of how bodies are used in caring for another's mind and how this undertaking can be read as physical suffering with a psychic cause. Foucault's *scenes of supervision* (Britzman, Guzel, and Harms, forthcoming) create a frame to return to a historical prototype of psychiatry where the absence of the psychiatrist acts as both a judgment and an authority unexpectedly at the center of the practice of psychiatry. This practice lacuna leads to questions of what psychiatry is for and what is at stake with a psychiatric practice reliant on the psychiatric body that is frequently out of reach but whose reach is felt by all. Finally, I reflect on my own practice encounters in child and youth mental health, recognizing that the contemporary scenarios of care are not so distant from Foucault's observations and necessarily situate questions about how it is that knowledge about the mind coalesces in a practice marked by the absence of the psychiatrist.

Chapter 5 moves more closely into autoethnography. I have spent a great deal of my professional life in two places: Canada and Uganda. I completed part of my postgraduate psychiatry training in Uganda, which led to a number of important professional and personal relationships. These relationships have led to unique opportunities to work and teach in psychiatric settings in Uganda. And it was in Uganda that I learned something can come from nothing. I observed how resource deficits are uniquely overcome by creativity and human tenacity. This attunement to nothingness highlighted my own state of mind, which was also frequently empty. It was in Uganda that I learned the fallacy of depending on what I thought I should know, only to find a conspicuous absence. I also discovered that I survived. The phrase *something comes from nothing* acts as an emotional harbinger and educational marker for the broader thematic of an educational void, encountered as a situational dilemma yet survived through this thought transformation. Chapter 5 therefore presents an autoethnographic narrative about my experience as a faculty educator in Uganda. However, the perspective shifts when I write myself into the field around the dilemma of trying to educate while simultaneously trying to unlearn my own education.

Throughout chapter 5, I turn to two main authors, Sally Swartz (2019) and Koichi Togashi (2020), who are both psychoanalysts and deeply engaged in thinking about decolonization in their clinical work. Swartz practices in South Africa and focuses on the notion of ruthlessness as a quality of human survival that is of no use unless it is a point of departure for a disrupted ordinary rendering a new self with agency and capability. I have borrowed generously from her insights and have used them in the service of trying to make sense of educational scenes where I was often at sea and rudderless. Togashi, who is Japanese, takes a decolonizing approach to psychoanalysis by critiquing psychoanalytic theory historically interpreted and aligned with the philosophical West. He explores a new ethical turn through a set of thought coordinates drawing on Eastern philosophy. Togashi offers a place of human intersubjectivity that transcends proscribed professional roles and explores new ways of engagement that underscore and anchor observations I am making in the service of unlearning education as an educator.

Emerging from a training largely rooted in empiricism and attempting to find another conceptual model to tackle the notion of an educator's education made from practice, chapter 6 considers the work of writing and the redemption inherent in it, proposing a way out from thinking that has performed a type of professional dead end for me, and paradoxically into a capacious intrasubjective confidence predicated on the vulnerability inherent in the natality of uncertainty and its educational possibilities.

One

Brittle Education

Deficiency Dialogues

Most people don't love the idea of coming to a psychiatrist, and apprehension typically paves the way into my office for all kinds of reasons. The one I hear most commonly from youth goes something like this:

Me: I'm glad to be able to get the chance to talk to you.

Adolescent: I'm not crazy, you know.

At the start of my practice, the adolescent's response caught me seriously off guard, and had me feeling like I had been outwitted in a game of my own making. In those early days of learning to be a child and adolescent psychiatrist, I would wait with nervous anticipation for the patient to show up in the clinic, smoothing down unwanted wrinkles on my clothes in a physical effort to appear like I imagined a physician would. I would comb through the patient's referral documents, jot down notes and organize interview prompts, think through creative ways of asking difficult questions, consult the literature for reassurance it couldn't give, move the chairs in the small office space and place them just so, ensure that Kleenex was readily available just in case, and then wait some more. This display of obsessive neurosis, albeit helpful at the time, was dependably present and experienced as the sensation of shallow breathing in a depleted atmosphere of my own making. Worry was everywhere. So it should not have come as a surprise to me that the first words from a youth were also expressions of worry. But the youth's statement about not wanting to be identified as crazy didn't worry me so much as the ways it marked a problematic interruption for me. I could tackle the problem of "crazy" so to speak, but I was less interested in this exploration, oddly enough, because I didn't think the term itself had anything to do with contemporary psychiatry. My worry had to do with an inconvenience of time in which the youth's agenda was in conflict with mine. The explorations of presumed insanity would require more time than I had, whereas I needed all the time I could get to painstakingly explore diagnostic symptoms that may or may not align with a narrative about losing one's mind. It wasn't only declarations of insanity that went sour in my early days of practice. As it turns out, there were many ways that the start of a child and adolescent psychiatrist appointment could get off on the wrong foot.

Another particular clinical experience I frequently encountered, which I have termed *the deficiency dialogue,* might go something like this: the desperate parent saying to their child or youth something like "Tell the doctor everything. Be honest. We can't help you if you don't talk" before stepping out of my office to ensure some private time with the psychiatrist. Looking back, I see now that there were two very different encounters that would await me during these private times. Compared to adolescents, children varied enormously in their reactions to meeting a doctor who was interested in how they felt, how they acted, and how they thought. Therefore, the interviews also transpired in dramatically dissimilar ways.

If the patient was a child, he or she would typically look ambivalent, blank, or a bit bored, generally unaware of the reason they were in a doctor's office. A veil of uncertainty about whether or not they could leave their seat and touch the toys scattered around the room was palpable for me, interrupting my own line of vision. I could sense the child's desire to explore the brightly colored objects, however it seemed to me that the children could easily intuit unspoken performance expectations from adults that required a rightfully earned invitation to play in an office not meant for it, instead of acting on their own innate, creative impulses. I have repeatedly watched the anticipated compliance that seemed unsettling in its reflexive ease for the young ones who entered my office. They frequently waited to be given outright permission to reach out for objects made precisely for small hands. Whatever anxiety was present for me in these encounters would momentarily be soothed by watching the little fingers wrap around the plastic figurines and contort them into shapes and characters and plot lines unknown to me. When I started clinical practice, I didn't yet feel comfortable giving the child permission to play. I sensed that this permission was in direct contrast to parental instruction, which was to sit still and clearly explain the problem to the doctor.

The adolescent youth is another story. Their serious anxiety or outright anger doubles as an office introduction. At this point, adolescent emotions become the organizing factor for a conversation oriented toward exposing personal suffering desperately meant to be kept a half-secret. Silence at this point, if present, is usually hostile. As it turns out, an averted gaze can be a precisely directed glare. And it is not lost on me that this prelude occurs long before the psychiatric interview has begun. Often hoodies would be pulled so tight over the youth's head with torsos slouched so far into the chair that it seemed plausible the floor could swallow them whole. Perhaps grounding was what was most precisely needed in that moment, although I hadn't recognized that possibility yet. Youth are often very clever in their silence, whether intended or not, forcing the embarrassed parent to say more than they want to in front of their youth. But who wants to waste the doctor's time? Someone has to talk. I would hear the parent's well-meaning concerns about the youth's isolation, aggression, avoidance, deterioration, body odor, irritability, or hostility spoken in front of the adolescent whose proposed embodiment of this list of negativities was simply intolerable, at least in that very moment. I can only say that it felt like watching gasoline being tossed onto a determined flame with no fire extinguisher in sight, and with the full knowledge of the emotional detonation to follow. In the moments after, if I could work with the youth to make it past the crying, screaming, defending, name calling, storming out, or refusal to move or speak, it was a good day.

The sensation of squirming in my seat would continue well beyond the initial moments of the patient encounter. There were many reasons to be uncomfortable back then, but at the heart of the matter was a crisis of identity. I was deeply unsettled by being mistaken for a therapist and would indicate as much. Just the parent's insistence that the child speak and, "Tell the doctor everything," was enough to get me itchy.

"No," I would say, "It's okay if Alexis doesn't feel like talking. Sometimes it's hard to say what's on our minds. And besides, I am not a counselor." My answer, although not intended as such, felt like ill-timed griping. At the time, I would have described it as a justification and an important redirection for those requiring education about what I did. A clear distinction existed in my understanding of roles. I had a serious task to complete in the form of diagnostics. How would the spilling of any guts help me to accomplish this? I wasn't trained in storytelling, which, after all, was far less relevant than the careful crafting required of me to arrive at symptomatic certainty. Whether or not these certainties were certain to provide relief to parent and child alike was a question I would deal with later. In other words, I would send the message to the parent and child that whatever story would be shared by them could be tolerated in exchange for the time required to get through my semistructured interview. It was a fair trade. Or, at least that's what I thought when I began practicing.

Another way of going back into this story of starting is to tell it again. But this time, the same story of a child and adolescent psychiatrist in the early days of practice is told with another disguise.

I sit in the corner of the hospital clinic room, in front of a computer, on a cushiony office chair the color of dirty gray with the possibility of a 360-degree swivel. Its uniqueness marks it as "the doctor's chair." I mostly like the chair because I feel that when I am in it, I may know a thing or two in order to be of help to someone. Perhaps the days that I need to remind myself of the significance of the chair coincide with the feeling that it would be easier if I were sitting in a different one. There are drawings made by my patients attached to the filing cabinet with magnets. Some of them have rainbows and flowers with "Thank you, Dr. Harms" printed in crayon. Another piece includes an eerie zombie-like figure, fingers long and ghoulish reaching around its own emaciated torso, grisly in aesthetic with evidence of pencils having been firmly pressed into the paper except for the illegible signature in the bottom right-hand corner of the page.

The parent and the young patient are seated not far from me, a small table between them. Large windows with blinds drawn are behind them, obscuring the view of the hospital courtyard that houses mini basketball nets and exercise machines intended for those sick enough to need reprieve from the locked mental health unit. Sometimes I wish I could play there. A spoken greeting occurs — the doctor, the patient, and the parent. I think I know what should happen next, but it doesn't go that way. Once again I hear a parent say to their child, "Tell the doctor everything. Be honest. We can't help you if you don't talk." I notice the way the parent leans over their youth or hovers around them, as though to signal with their bodies that they mean parental business. Serious business. I have no idea what business they are referring to, yet I have a sickish sense about it. Without warning, I am doing a dance where I vaguely know the steps, and sitting it out is not an option. I wonder if this is the moment to get up and go to the printer outside my office door. But I know I can't or shouldn't and so I don't. An urgency can be felt in the parental posturing and spoken words, registering more like a desperate plea or a stern command as opposed to a suggestion or even a casual request. Over the years, I have come to understand that there is nothing casual about this exchange. I perceive myself as an unwelcome visitor, a voyeur of sorts, watching a moment where the parent's tone suggests that the youth is being chastised about something they said or didn't say but I can't make out if the problem is in the moment or having to do with something that has nothing to do with my office. One thing is certain. The parents are deeply suspicious of what will happen if the teen does not speak. Danger lurks. And I wonder, who is it that's most afraid?

What I make of it in the moment is a clear signal for me to do the impossible. Implied in the parent's admonishment is the notion that an absolute truth can be absolutely and accurately told by the youth about their world while they are developmentally changing in response to it, and that once these rare gems are dug up and dusted off, it will be obvious to me what the singular cause of the problem is, and that I can then efficiently fix whatever suffering is plaguing the youth. It feels as though the task that needs to be completed is painfully clear to the parent, while I remain in the dark. I hear their unspoken request (rephrased in the most vernacular of ways), which lands more like a directive for me: "I brought my kid to you. Now make the pain go away." Awkward silence ensues. And while I would either say nothing or move on to a discussion about banal clinical details unrelated to the question at hand, my mind would implode with childish retaliations. My thought world would suddenly be consumed with a parallel shouting match that would go something like this: *But wait! How is this pain my problem? I had nothing to do with what happened before! Did you just hand me your child's suffering? You all need psychical emergency first aid! How could you wait THIS LONG to find a doctor? I am not at all prepared for this!"* These demanding, unspoken questions were silently screamed at the parent while I would continue the clinical encounter, hopefully without any indication of the ill-tempered mental war that raged within. The moments surrounding this guilty encounter would feel like a profound weight pressing on me that I was highly suspicious of my agility to crawl out from under, no matter how much effort I gave to escape. This resentful experience would also register as a vestigial deal gone badly. To be specific, the deal that ends with me "fixing" the child was made behind my back. But in the end, it seems as though someone has to pay for all of the suffering because no one has paid. Do I have the psychological spinal cord to stand up in this scene and redraw parameters that we can all live with but don't necessarily like?

The story keeps changing, scenes shift, perspectives turn, moving slightly out of the line of vision and somehow at the same time seriously getting under my skin. At first glance, there is an avalanche of socialization of what we imagine a psychiatrist says and does. It is a place that is filled with the fragments of a scene that has broken down because, oddly enough, it is a place that seems to disregard or deny the patient. If the patient does not cooperate with me, I can't do my job. And if I can't do my job, what am I doing here? And now it is the physician that requires saving. An odd turn of events, indeed.

How Should It Be?

As I step away from this scene, I am aware of the interest in the experiences of those who are insiders in medicine and what kind of education shapes clinical practice. Suffering and healing are, after all, deeply relatable human conditions. But at the time of starting medical practice, it felt as though every moment was dedicated toward an idea of how psychiatry should be, as loosely formed as those ideas were back then. I frequently felt as though I entered into a kind of hostile medical drama, and perhaps the most unsettling questions had to do with not really knowing what it was that the doctor was supposed to do or how I was to respond to stories when stories weren't really going to help me. These queries originally registered for me as unspeakable and were iteratively compressed into a specific space made up of unanswered questions. Here, in this new space where queries go to live or die, a new organ formed in the small of my self, and its evolutionary purpose was to help me survive medicine. That organ is called "I don't know if I can help." It would be some time before I understood how my work, intended to help relieve suffering minds, had become so conflated with a strange kind of risk that presented itself at the start of each interview and then lingered for me. It would also be a long time before I recognized the critical educational importance of sensing the fear and anxiety of the parents as a signal that could find me alive to more generative ideas.

Spectacular Failures

I can see now that the problems I am referring to can be conceptualized as educational in nature. I am trying to understand what is going on and simultaneously attempting to paradoxically explain what I am not or what I don't do as a child and adolescent psychiatrist. I am really interested in knowing how it is that things get so easily derailed and often end up in spectacular failures such that things get bent out of shape before I even start to do my job. And attempting to explain why I can't do something requires an understanding, and therein lies part of the education problem. Learning is difficult to define but I have come to understand it for myself as deeply personal, with a type of psychical disassembling constituted by thinking away from my thoughts, leaving fragments as unfinished business, often registering only as niggling discomforts or attention barely placed at something that almost caught my eye but won't leave my mind. The estranging, intimate, and occasionally tortuous process of putting things back together again is where my mind is changed. Similarly, returning to my psychiatry office scenes, the shattering of its presumed coherence naturally leads to attempts at making sense or coming up with interpretations about a situation headed toward unanticipated conflict. In doing so, the scenario itself instructs but also can be thought of as the site of education in order to determine what has been made, what has been inherited, and, perhaps most importantly, what has been felt.

Paradoxically, as a psychiatrist, I was wary of emotions as having any instructional value, despite the popular belief that psychiatry is an emotional domain. Simple clinical errors signaled a possibility for education to come to the fore through a lopsided, affecting space where mistakes would register. Not knowing how to respond, or recognizing that the patient was unhappy with what I had to say, or that the patient was angry in response to my comments, suggested that education is discursively associated with a discourse on feelings. A kaleidoscope was created from these errors when the situation wasn't right. Instead of education being a space of opening for me, it was often responsible for a closing down. If I could interpret my clinic scene a different way, it's like I hated my feelings and had the sense that those coming to me for their own emotional reprieve hated them too. Soothing myself with overwrought logistics and procedures to convince myself that I had not fallen apart in a job where the impossible task at hand was to get the job done pointed to a psychical frenzy. But what had become clear for me was that my own thoughts and expectations were at odds with what actually happened in a psychiatry office. Questions emerging from my office experience such as "Who are you?" "Where am I?" "Who is talking?" and "Does the silence matter?" have continued to creep through the storied cracks between the doctor and the patient, replete with the anticipation of both parties arriving at satisfied certainty. However, the predictable promise of falling apart frequently was the last word, despite best efforts. Otherwise said, the education can't contain, or ignores or obliterates, the capacity to imagine mistakes. By placing my experience at the center of the problem of education, what was never intended to be education is now education. As I have learned, the world of mental health is far more complicated because we all subjects responding to mental life.

Practitioners in Mind

There are a number of problems that go into the making of a practitioner of the mind (by this I mean me, a psychiatrist). Describing the start to my psychiatry training may provide a glimpse into my hopes and desires coming into medical practice and where they eventually landed. When I entered residency training, I was deeply convinced of the possibility of psychiatry as an accessible space for human pain and believed the field was generative, tolerant, and open to locating humanity in both healer and patient alike. In many ways, I wanted the practice of learning psychiatry to be a counteragent to my experience in medical school, where I had become thoroughly convinced of my intractable stupidity. I will return to the idea of personal idiocy later. I found it a relief to be in the specialty where I was more at home and where I wanted to be. But demands of many kinds were made of me during this time, intellectual as well as emotional, to embrace facts and clinical perspectives when I still felt unsure. The certainty that I observed in my fellow learners and teachers consolidated for me the idea of being an expert, leaving me with doubts about my own possible expertise and wondering if I belonged in such a confident culture. For example, I was immersed in a consultation system requiring efficient articulation of both the psychiatric problem and the evidence-based plan in a succinct note after a visit that would last anywhere between thirty minutes to an hour. The referring physician would receive our consultation note after we had completed the assessment, or at least that's the assumption that was made, and our job as consulting psychiatrists would be done. I was aware that patients' emotional pain could not easily be conceptualized in a consultation paradigm where, after one visit, the expectation was that I had come to a correct diagnosis and that the sharing of this diagnosis and a treatment plan that I would not follow through with would somehow soothe and mend. Over time, delivering to the patient and the family the parting sentence, "I will send my report to your family doctor describing all the things we have talked about and they can follow up," felt as though I was betraying everyone, including my family medicine colleagues who were the ones to most commonly make referrals to psychiatry. Later, after I had learned to take my time, or at least as much time as I felt was needed, my patients' recurring critiques of previous encounters with physicians attempting to do what I had been trained to do told me my discomfort was justified. They would say about the last psychiatrist, "He only spent twenty minutes with me. How can anyone know me in that amount of time? He just told me to take a pill but I didn't do it because I didn't believe what the doctor said." It was like I was being followed by a cloud of discontent that pointed to something I could not put my finger on. I had excellent preceptors during training and worked in a system that, in all regards, was an example of good psychiatric practice. Yet I was at odds with the practice of psychiatry, and it seemed as though my patients were too.

But I could often explain away the challenges, stating that it was the patients who were unhappy. Patients could be seen as noncompliant, oppositional, or resistant to personal work that needed to be done, or whatever label could be pasted to the patient's back indicating that the problem was theirs and they should just stand in the corner until they realized what they had done wrong. And then they would spend another nine months on a waiting list to get back into the very clinic that had discharged them. The patient's failure to show up for an appointment could easily been seen as their fault and would readily create a justification for discharging them. Of course, discharging patients when they did not attend appointments wasn't always what happened, but it happened in this way enough times to stick in my memory such that I needed to come back to it over and over again as a kind of knot in my body that wouldn't stop aching. I now understand why, at the time, I couldn't speak of these challenges. As it turns out, I can't comment on my development as I am developing, in the same way the teens in my clinic who are asked to "be honest and tell the doctor everything" can only tell what they can. And the interesting observation here is that while there are many obstacles to contend with, I often can't tell the difference between obstacles to learning and obstacles within me.

During psychiatry residency training, we didn't get tested per se, but there was a final exam we were all working toward. Interestingly, the ultimate proof of success came in the form of a certificate from the Royal College of Physicians and Surgeons (RCPSC) of Canada — a credentialing authority whose robust testing methods did not directly rely on observed patient encounters. I am not being sarcastic here. The evaluation methods at the RCPSC are extremely rigorous, arguably world-class. However, when the time came, my passing scores on this standardized test and the resulting achievement of RCPSC professional credentials did not touch on the sticky situations I would iteratively encounter with patients, signaling an expertise about the working of the mind that I did not feel. It left me wondering who or what would be the ultimate adjudicator if my own expert authority faltered? And my early attempts at outpatient care as a qualified child and adolescent psychiatrist were often not any more successful than the venerated consultation model I had learned in residency. What I continued to discover through a presumed practice of healing were problems I was working through educationally. As I said earlier, the *know-how* in the custodianship of care neither readily nor easily translated into *show how*.

For example, how could I reassure a desperate parent who had just discovered that her daughter, barely out of childhood, had delicately and precisely carved the words "kill me" into the long of her forearms? I too was queasy at seeing this dermal epitaph of deliberate self-harm and felt as though the shock of discovering it sabotaged the tools and strategies I was taught to reliably deploy to understand what led to the moment. Cutting as a form of soothing or as an act of self-punishment has a profoundly reinforcing neurobiological cascade deeply resistant to change. What kind of emotional salve could be prescribed to replace the need to bleed? How could I cogently explain this kind of dizzying trauma to the patient's mother, whose job it was to protect her daughter's body and mind? Similarly, how could I convince a confused mother that there is real hope for a future following her teenage daughter's anxious revelation that the way that she carried her arm in gym was not because of a neurological deficit but because it intentionally mimicked the posture of a dinosaur claw? Until the moment of the psychiatric interview, the adolescent had never been able to say to her mother that she felt much more at home with the belief that her body belonged to that of a prehistoric reptile.

Not all encounters in those early days ended with dread and disorientation. Some patient encounters led me to experiences of textbook achievements such as the pharmacological treatment of anxiety or psychosis, or prescribing Ritalin to the inattentive, hyperactive boy whose impulsive and targeted aggression cleared his classroom. But in the case of the overactive boy, the residue of a historical, monstrous identity capable of inciting the catastrophic urgency of a school fire drill never really dissipated for him, leaving behind a social solemnity more problematic than his swinging fists.

More often, deep places of confusion about what was really happening to me and around me were subdued by an education primarily predicated on taxonomies of symptoms. My seemingly correct diagnostic interpretations were hardly corrective, even when the psychiatric problem appeared "simple." No treatment algorithm for the exceptionally bright young man who felt that he was born into the wrong gender could help me respond to his pain. Alternatively, his attempts at relieving suffering in the form of repeatedly swallowing handfuls of pills were declared by him to be the most effective in providing what was needed most in intolerable moments. My expertise was rendered relatively obsolete in comparison to the numbing effect of countless capsules. Displays of professional certainty within these patient engagements often registered for me as premature, sterile, and distressing, and at times it felt as though I was foreclosing on the complexities inherent in the fragility and unknowability of psychical life.

What Is Education Made Of?

Up to this point, I have provided a glimpse into some of my early clinical experiences as a child and adolescent psychiatrist, as well as the education that came before and has since emerged. Through my descriptions of what appears to be my education in psychiatry acting on the patient, another question clearly emerges. What does an education in psychiatry do to a psychiatrist? While it may seem like an odd question, isn't it the odd and slightly off that capture our attention? I cannot take credit for this question — it has been borrowed from sociologist Willard Waller (2014) and retrofitted here for psychiatry. When I speak of education, I continue to challenge what is historically or traditionally associated with the term: curriculum, classrooms, tests, grades, recess, and lunchtime. Rather, I am trying to turn away from the traditional path of symptom identification, diagnosis, and treatment and get intentionally lost so that creativity and the imaginary are invited to help reimagine what constitutes education. The act of trying to imagine education differently often took the form of traditional learning, which included reading, studying, seeing patients, and so on but also included being alive to the emotional clues within me that were experienced as a sensation of being "pressed upon." These clues could be thought of as replacing a formal curriculum such that the task at hand was precisely to make meaning of what was happening or had happened, relying on my internal clues. Looking back, the only vectors of meaning I could identify at the time were affect. But affect can be tricky to speak of, because it can signal an emotional influence as much as an effect. In order to unpack the experience of affect as education, it was as if I needed to reach into a kind of imaginary similar to a dreamlike state, to access what it is that I am trying to talk about in relationship to education.

But perhaps what emerges from my query about what an education in psychiatry does to a psychiatrist includes viewing my medical education experience as a series of dilemmas. Education has taken on a number of valences for me: an education in a learning profession, an education made from psychiatric practice working with children and adolescents, and an education of an educator. Each of these learning fragments has required of me expert knowledge and skills, simultaneously creating conditions where both knowledge and caring are paradoxically insufficient or doubted. Here, the maelstrom of problems, as well as an inability to say with specificity when I (or anyone else for that matter) am occupying a particular role, begins to signal the confluence as an educational marker. And by this, I mean the dependable problem of intersubjective collisions inherent in patient and teaching encounters, bringing to bear histories from patient, student, and healer alike, inevitably resulting in rich layers of human complexity not readily amenable to textbook answers. Like the Tower of Babel, people and their situations, as well as their histories, are talking, sometimes to each other, with the expectation that communication will be successful. However, the problem is in the transmission. All goes predictably haywire.

Sigmund Freud (1964) gives us some very particular antidotes to thinking about or thinking in conflicts. He would suggest that clarity is possible within the chaos of problems through a process of imagination otherwise known as free association. Saying what is on one's mind can be of service when one can't be of service to oneself. Similarly, Deborah Britzman (2003a) gives us insight into why Freud's "fundamental rule" of free association can be a tortuous one. She describes the exercise as an opportunity for the analysand to speak of conflicts that arise but adds that "this experience of conflict allows for all that will follow, not just in the analytic setting, although it is there where free association may matter most, but also something like free association can take residence in the pedagogical imagination, where there, too, the fragility of language gives notice to the difficulty of freely associating and the utter importance of doing just that" (25). Relying then on this invitation for thought departures, what comes to mind when imagining a teaching scenario in child and adolescent psychiatry? Who is present? What is said? What happens? How does it feel? Where is the exit?

I have also taken up the idea of free associating as a pedagogical tool with psychiatry residents in training, but only as of late. I have found that that experiential quality of free associating has the possibility of preparing us for what we can never fully be prepared for when it comes to human encounters. And this is an important harbinger of the lack that constitutes medical education and the practice that will come of it. I will share with you a brief illustration taken directly from my role as a clinical educator that speaks to this space of deficiency as well as to the convergence of the educational valences I speak of above: an education in a learning profession, an education made from psychiatric practice working with children and adolescents, and an education of an educator.

Into the Emergency

Join me in the psychiatry emergency department where I frequently work and teach. One of the most common reasons a youth is referred to me is for a "risk assessment," which may suggest any number of concerning behaviors on the part of the youth, including aggression, suicidal gestures, and threats of self-harm, to name a few. But the common problems that I encounter in this setting do not typically share the same outcomes, and the scene I am about to bring you into is an example of what happens with an anticipated problem and its unanticipated results.

In this scene, I am supervising a psychiatry resident and we are talking about the different reasons a youth may be aggressive, leading to a visit at our emergency department. The resident I am working with is astute and can easily come up with any number of psychiatric as well as nonpsychiatric causes for unmitigated, outward expressions of sadness, disappointment, trauma, and anxiety all neatly rolled up into a ball of dangerous unpredictability. We talk about this convergence of affect, anticipate the patient's various responses, and in particular review what the student is learning about establishing therapeutic rapport. Conveying an openness to listening is essential, particularly with a young person who likely feels as though she is without a voice, suggests the resident. Nonetheless, our job is to determine how much the youth poses a risk to themselves or to others in order to think about next steps. My student looks confident but sounds somewhat nervous. We talk about what it means to listen to the patient and what it means to listen to ourselves. I suggest that sometimes it is hard to distinguish between the two. We agree that the student will take the lead in interviewing. We also negotiate a universal sign of distress for the resident in the event that they feel overwhelmed and are unable to keep the conversation going, which amounts to this: "Dr. Harms, I wonder if you have any questions?" Got it. I will take over when I hear the resident ask this question in the interview. We have a plan, I say. Are you ready to go in? I ask. Yup, says the resident. Let's go.

We enter the psychiatry emergency patient room, which looks more like a prison cell than it should. There is a human figure lying still under hospital blankets, covered from head to toe. I can see the resident looking for chest wall movement to ensure the patient is not dead. Chest wall motion noted. Check. Things are going well, so far.

> RESIDENT: Hello? Hello? Hello? Sally? Can you hear me? Um, it's really nice to meet you. I am um, Dr. X, a resident in psychiatry who is working with Dr. Harms today in, um, the Emergency Department. I was hoping that we could, um, chat for a little while, to get to know you, to listen to what has been going on for you and um, to try and help you with . . .
>
> PATIENT: (*Violent kick under the blanket followed by stillness.*) *Resident looks to me and I give them a look that says it's okay to continue. The resident uses the therapeutic tone of voice and language they have been taught to use.*
>
> RESIDENT: Like I was saying, we are really glad to be able to meet you and, um, get to know you. I have read your chart and, um, know a bit about what brought you into hospital. I won't ask you to tell me your whole story again because I suspect that would, um, be really frustrating for you. I know that this is a tough time in your life. Um, can you tell us in your own words what happened to bring you to hospital?
>
> PATIENT: Don't treat me like a fucking baby with your stupid-ass counselor voice. You don't know anything about me. Fuck off and get me the fuck out of here.
>
> RESIDENT: (*Long pause.*) Dr. Harms, I wonder if you have any questions?
>
> DR. HARMS: Sure. Being in the hospital is totally the worst. Let's try to get you out.
>
> PATIENT: Then fucking let me leave.
>
> DR. HARMS: We do need to talk first.
>
> PATIENT: I told you to fuck off. NOW DO IT!
>
> DR. HARMS: We've heard you. We'll leave and come back later.
>
> *Dr. Harms and resident exit the patient's room and close the door quietly behind them.*

For the reader, there is an advantage in being able to follow the above script to help orient the scene and the order of speakers, as though it has a logical sequence. But if our eyes are closed and we cannot read the speaker cues or their assigned tasks, we could easily imagine an interchange in the mix of shouting and begging, stumbling of speech, unwanted instructions, escape fantasies or demands to be elsewhere, suspending time with silence, as well as being tongue-tied. The teacher learning to teach, the student learning to learn, and the patient waiting to be healed can be seen as one and the same, although deeply varied in how each personal history arrived on the clinical stage. This scene and its dramatics is one reason why Freud (1964) referred to medicine as one of the impossible professions in its ultimate promise of dissatisfaction, where the limits of professional practice are also experienced by those who practice within it. Nobody in my educational scene was happy, healed, or repaired. But we were all affected by discontent. Britzman (2009) tells us that a profession like psychiatry is impossible "because it proposes a constitutive discontinuity, a lack the profession represses, negates, and projects into others" (129).

It is interesting to consider the impossible professions and simultaneously think about the idea of "proof" underpinning the certainty of medicine. When I was in medical school, the term "evidence-based medicine" was nothing short of intellectually hot. If you wanted to sound legitimate, you would be the one in any rounds or teaching session or bedside encounter to posit the question, "What does the evidence say?" And in participating in this kind of iterative event, either consciously or unconsciously, my confidence in medicine was not only bolstered but over time cemented as a rock-solid, sure thing. I had evidence on my side; an uncontested fact that could double as biblical truth (if one believes in chapter and verse, that is). I was grateful for a certainty that would steady me in a time that often felt as though I had lost my footing. I therefore entered into psychiatry training, already replete with paradigms supporting my empirical convictions that felt more like transcendental faith. The message during psychiatry training was that the field was approaching biological certainties, rendering the brain possibly predictable and knowable, and that this certainty would be scientifically illuminated through biomarkers and neuroimaging.

Despite this, I still often found myself ill-prepared to explore the conceptions of the mind, and at times became antagonistically oriented toward a failed professional promise of understanding. It seemed so easy when I watched skilled psychiatrists at work. But this observed ease was at odds with what I felt or thought was easy. I increasingly experienced myself as both cause and effect of this failed profession, unsuccessful within a mandate to understand the mind and its proclivity toward brokenness, thereby giving up frequently and foreclosing on an interest in the mind's "emotional antics." This is how I survived. Furthermore, I would frequently recognize my own quiet hostility directed at others: colleagues, patients, and family members alike, who would ask for answers to questions I could not articulate, let alone understand.

Daniel Carlat (2010) weighs in on this kind of vitriol, describing the psychiatric profession as having reached a crisis point such that a collective professional paralysis has ensued in the wake of psychopharmacology and its capitalistic agendas and allegiances. Over time, I came to understand what Carlat was saying; the practice of psychiatry often resonated like a one-trick pony in its pharmacology-heavy focus. If a pill couldn't fix the problem, it signaled a personal ineffectiveness. Most of the research evidence we reviewed in training specifically had to do with being able to recite how effective pill A was versus pill B in a variety of psychiatric conditions. But we were also responsible for knowing many ways in which the whole person could heal. And while I theoretically knew there were many modes of recovery, the modality associated with the "talking cure" did not really seem to register with equal clout. I sensed that talk therapy was for others whose scope of practice was not as important as the need for diagnostics and medical interpretation or treatment. Perhaps as a consequence, I had also developed a kind of medical myopia in not seeing psychiatry's emotionality or the potential for it, fostering a kind of automated engagement where I would rely on capsules, taxonomies, and metrics, which would later translate into uncomfortable emotional symptoms about my education that would demand reckoning. I discovered later that any intellectual poverty I experienced as a psychiatrist or psychiatry educator could readily be exchanged for the enamor of belonging to a professional group presumed to be secure in its empirical confidence.

Negative Capability

For me, learning is usually an approach toward a tenuous border of knowing or know-how. It seems that my struggle has more to do with the mottled, confused, and silent moments of my affected response to knowledge uncertainty rather than the elusive nature of learning itself. The distinction between the two is critical in understanding my own educational condition. Indeed, Darian Leader (2012) highlights a quiet psychotic trajectory as one that is qualitatively more attuned to camouflaging an underlying paranoia by hiding pressing queries that arise internally. At the same time, our behavior conforms to expectations, and we demonstrate compliance as a tacit recognition that the suppression of any outward signs of psychosis is key. Leader contrasts this to the outward forms of psychosis that would be readily understood by the majority as "mad" — that is the striking nonsensical symptomatology of what is seen to be bizarre, disorganized, and sometimes violent. The descriptive proximity of quiet psychosis to my educational experience where my affected response to the unknown proves more problematic than a lack of knowledge is a provocative one for me, although I suspect that those around me would not have observed any outward indication that my inward thinking was at odds with the medical world around me.

John Keats (1988) coined the term "negative capability" when he described the qualities of a successful writer as having the staying power to remain firmly within the possibility offered by mystery without the grasp of certainty. The description offered by Keats inspired other thinkers such as Wilfred Bion (1970), who expanded on this idea, describing negative capability as a critical ability to tolerate the unknown. Both of these descriptions resemble the place of working through offered by Leader (2012). The pinpoint location of *unknown* becomes the educational coordinates of working through. Here, in the void, the idea of *lack* becomes generative. Britzman (2024) expands on Bion's idea by describing what uncertainty opens or emotionally permits and how it can be used in the service of education. She describes negative capability as "our finest resource for working through the schizoid defenses and their denial of the relational, infantile roots of the emotional world" (160). In this way, the capacity to enter into the unknown, that is to speak beyond the answers provided in medical texts and positivistic data, points to a constitutive fragility inherent in the work of engaging my education as a potentially feeble or frenetic place, yet also signals an ineffable potential requiring time for possible and recognizable transformation.

While it is uncomfortable to admit, a perceived failure of knowledge as a child and adolescent psychiatrist has frequently animated in me a resisting internal conflict where uncertainty at times performed a shameful behavioral response of unsettled confusion directed against my patients. While I was taught that my confusion would be assuaged by the empiricism of evidence-based practice that I mentioned earlier, in reality the authority of evidence was frequently used to close conversations rather than open them up. I would say things to my patients like "The research says that drug X is the best medication to try at this point," thinking that this declaration of knowledge would settle the patient as much as the knowledge of the fact settled me. It was the best psychiatry had in terms of knowledge, a trump card of sorts, even if the best was not good enough to help me in the patient situations in which I frequently found myself. The more I relied on my training, the more best practice guidelines left me at a loss in understanding how to efficiently and cogently disentangle the layers of traumatic loss, painful desires, creative potential, temporality, and idealized longings that penetrate adolescent life. Proposing beneficent interventions often felt like an afterthought.

In the experiences above, it seemed that my education in psychiatry had broken down for me, demanding a type of internal tactical retaliation where my adolescent patients became the target in my mind's eye. I would allow myself to think statements that I continue to hear to this day, either directly or inferred: Whatever problem the patient is experiencing has nothing to do with me; suffering is the fault of the patient or the family or the school system or the economy or the environment, and any other list of variables that can be reasonably called upon. The list of castigations was endless and necessary to soothe me, acting as a justifiable mitigation when acknowledging my own perceived professional inadequacies. Blame felt better than the shame of not knowing. Neither felt good.

Curiously, it would be Freud who offered me a novel lexicon of psychoanalytic terms to help me explore this emotional battleground in his work with the unconscious and its drives. Freud's premise in his famous "talking cure" was that honesty about our motives, our desires, and subsequently our emotions does not come easy to us. According to Freud (1964), our discomfort is a perfect hiding spot for our unconscious that then requires us to rely on the unspoken, parapraxis, common forgettings, and slips of the tongue to speak what has not been spoken. It is not difficult for me to see how this phenomenon can easily be applied to my shameful vengeful thoughts and responses.

Building on Freud's ideas about emotionally oriented language, D. W. Winnicott (2014) also appeared to be alive to my educational situation as an analyst. He recognized that an inevitable emotional storm warning was required when psychiatrists were in the presence of their patients, although it was likely a state of unawares that would catch most of us in the profession off guard. He states, "However much he [the psychiatrist] loves his patients, he cannot avoid hating them and fearing them, and the better he knows this, the less will hate and fear be the motives determining what he does to his patients" (195).

The lecture I like to call "Why I Hate My Patients" was absent from the psychiatry curriculum I was exposed to, presumably because any of the Freudian techniques that we did study were generally tolerated as historical artifacts. Freud's ideas were hardly used for anything other than references to dirty jokes. However, discovering anew the work of Freud, whose ideas could be used as deeply generative ways of probing uncertainties and misunderstandings I was tackling in the work of learning, was nothing short of transformative. Freud understood my encounters with patients as a transference problem. Britzman (2011) describes transference as when "the wandering mind drifts through long ago relations and fixates, obsesses, and forgets them" (2) and then unconsciously resurfaces to comment on present day troubles. Psychoanalytic ideas had come to bear on my medical education such that patients and their families were then readily referred to as "difficult" and secondary to failures of my own understanding. I felt justified using this "difficult" title in the wake of my failure. That is, a perceived professional minimization occurred in which it felt as though my compromised competency was publicly declared, even though the castigation occurred only in my mind. Through the status of my intense affect, the difficult patient signals for me the intolerable somatic embodiment of difficult knowledge, described by Alice Pitt and Deborah Britzman (2003) as "a concept meant to signify both representations of social trauma in curriculum and the individual's encounter with them in pedagogy" (755). The concept of difficult knowledge articulated the problem I had encountered in the uncertain education of psychiatry. I found myself on a fault line where the divide between the idea of education and what has never been thought of as education was a chasm worth going into.

In summary, in my intentional plunge into this murky chasm I am trying to enter into a kind of investigation into the status of uncertainty in medical education, the anxiety and emotional logic that come to bear on learning as a practitioner of psychiatry, and where the case of difficult knowledge is a signal of the implicit affective reasoning within education. This chasm is also where I attempt to engage the obstacles to understanding education. Before concluding,

I want to provide a bit of a map to help frame an understanding of my own journey and how my path was not trodden alone. I have colleagues who have explored similar situations and questions, and one colleague in particular, I met through reading and writing. I will iteratively return to his work, as well as the work of others, in exploring my question about what an education in psychiatry does to a psychiatrist.

About Trauma and Oliver Sacks

Much of my time in the emergency department is spent with adolescent girls who have experienced sexual trauma. It is not surprising that for these young women, being alone is when they are most afraid, most vulnerable, and when emotions loom large. The setting of the sun does not help because the loss of light deprives them of a critical tool to clearly see their attacker, who now resides in their minds and in their bodies. My goal in working with them is to explore different kinds of scripts over time. Here is what I might say:

> Focusing on your protection, being protected, and having access to places that will protect you is important. Eventually you can trust yourself to be safe enough with your own mind, even if your attacker has found a comfortable corner to hang out in it. These attackers turned intruders predictably go deep into our minds, and they tend to preferentially set up shop in the anatomy of our amygdala or the hippocampus. These are the places in your brain where emotions and memories come together. Attackers are unwisely brave and leave their hiding place in your mind and wander around in your body, because they think they own you. But you know enough about your body, or you will come to know it over time, so you can locate them and place a lock on their door, stopping them from wandering around. You can give them firm instructions about how you want them to behave. If they don't listen now, they will learn. You can also unlock their door and demand that they leave, even for a little while. Attacking intruders do eventually leave for good, but sometimes they come back. Sometimes, they remain with us. In this situation, you can still be very okay because eventually we can't tell ourselves apart from them, and this is a reality we can live with.

Then comes the terrifying work of living out this tidy trope. In hindsight, I needed this kind of therapeutic framework during medical school and residency to prepare me for what felt were unwelcome thought intrusions that I would need to contend with in deep and personal ways. I do have many memories of fun, joy, intellectual stimulation, and the excitement of being alive to new learning as well as being filled with a deep gratitude for the privilege of being with people at their most unwell. However, these memories are also coupled with experiences of being frightened, confused, disoriented, and not infrequently shamed, which seemed to suppress not only my capacity to think but also my drive to do so. When I stumbled onto Sacks's (2016) writing of his memoir *On the Move: A Life*, it was like I had found the residency partner and educational mentor I had always wanted. I had also found a voice to reach myself, long after the fact, but just in time. Sacks was the one who allowed me a vulnerable path back into my medical school and residency, and his writing acted as a banister for me to steady myself, repeatedly, to go back and make sense of what had not made sense earlier. Through his writing, Sacks took my hand and led me away from my amygdala to my prefrontal cortex and then gave me permission to roam where I would, even if meant returning to the wilds of working with the amygdala. Nothing was off-limits. I could easily imagine myself into scenarios where I was on his team, and he was the senior resident and I was the junior resident. We were in it together as learners, but he had enough tenacity, smarts, courageous disregard, and more than enough likability to grow out of his training. He seemed to have a unique kind of grit where he could admit failure and still find his feet when he was flat on the ground.

Sacks's brilliance lies in simple yet elegant descriptions of encountering life situations, some dramatic and many unanticipated, which I consider educational in nature, and where losing one's mind (and I think Sacks would say that he did) is the only viable option. Yet Sacks still comes out as a thinking person. How is this so? His memoir is an exemplar of an embodied question that organizes many of my queries and reflections as I explore various obstacles to conceptualizing the problems of education. His writing brings into somatic and psychical focus experiences I deeply resonate with, and some where I need to enter into an imaginary. For example, despite his described identity as a gay, British, white, Jewish male who grew up in the of post–World War II era, and who ended up in an American residency to study the brain, he found that he was always engaged in discussions of the mind, including his own. But when I read alongside him, the narrative is never clear or linear or straightforward. The fear factor is omnipresent in the way that he describes ominous experiences that he has overcome, although the reader often feels as though Sacks's past is returning to comment on the present. If anxiety could speak in Sacks's residency, I suspect it would say (among other things), "If I think about problems, I don't know what I am doing." And having completed training, I can now understand this as the heroic side of medicine in which pretending that we know acts as a salient defense against the uncertainty that most of us face in critical circumstances. Throughout this book, you will find me working alongside Sacks's writing, thinking about what he is not saying in his memoir in order to imagine myself in places where I could not go in my own medical education.

Two

Riding Pillion with Oliver Sacks

I have something in common with Oliver Sacks. We have both undergone a medical education that grapples with questions of the human mind, although Sacks specialized in neurology whereas I trained to be a psychiatrist with expertise in the mental health of children and adolescents. In his memoir *On the Move: A Life*, Sacks (2016) comes to the conclusion that his irreverent practice of neurology demanded the recognition of psychical life inherent in emotional pain, traditionally tended to by psychiatrists. He saw himself occupying space within both of these medical specialties, despite the crippling stigma often associated with psychiatry. He said, "When I was a resident at UCLA, neurology and psychiatry were presented as almost unrelated disciplines, but when I emerged from residency to encounter the full reality of patients, I often found I had to be as much a psychiatrist as a neurologist" (174). In doing so, Sacks's declaration of his dual identity signals a personal tenacity in which the storied intimacies he offers led to a different kind of thinking about medical training and professional practice, precisely as an educational case understood through personal narrative or memoir. But his memoir also signals a different kind of medical education. Sacks's reflections create the affecting conditions in which his written recollection of an education deeply marked by human desire and nonconformist thoughts will drive his intense creativity, prolific writing, and emotional struggle, which make way for what was often troubling in his elusive search of himself through education. An educational inquiry emerges from Sacks's writing about how he affected his own medical education and practice. His deeply vulnerable account invites a close reading of his life as an educational narrative informed by psychoanalysis, a tradition that Sacks engaged for over fifty years. I wonder if Sacks would say that his long-term engagement with the talking cure saved him from the brink of no return, and in doing so, perhaps inadvertently fueled his wildly successful and unconventional writing within a medical establishment often antagonistically oriented toward him. Through his writing, Sacks provides a number of different accounts of his education that I have read as an educational exemplar from the vantage point of a psychiatrist attempting to make sense of my own medical education.

I too rely on psychoanalysis, or rather psychoanalytic orientations, to arrive at some of the narrative themes figuring prominently in my experience of medical education. Sacks acted as the thematic navigator for me in offering up his generative stories. I found the many scenes where he describes attempts to hide himself in medicine, or to deconstruct/reconstruct himself to be a palatable medical subject of learning, are scenes constantly at play in both of our experiences. I use Sacks's account as a kind of thought banister, relying on the experiences narrated by Sacks to explore questions having to do with education, including educational origins. When is it that medical education really begins? And if I read Sacks as an antiphonal event to make sense of my own experience, when did my psychiatric education begin, recognizing that the muddled, intertwining of moments may neither be readily nor easily distinguishable? How then do we understand the registers of time that seem out of place in their before- and aftereffects? In this growing pyramid of questions, I turn to thinking about what resources were discovered or abandoned in the stifling experience of uncertainty and helplessness. And perhaps most saliently, I consider what happens when learning is traumatic and registers as a gnawing sense that seeks reprieve through unlearning.

In the Beginning

What happens before medical school? Sacks tells us he was trapped. Writing about his early school experiences, Sacks (2016) laments, "When I was at boarding school, sent away during the war as a little boy, I had a sense of imprisonment and powerlessness, and I longed for movement and power, ease of movement and superhuman powers" (3). Confinement and desire are coupled for Sacks, suggesting emotional bricks and mortar that will form the story of his early school days within another broader story about education, eloquently written into his memoir. Sacks has a ready antidote to his early academic asylum; it is an affecting logic that he will return to again and again, describing phenomenologically what something is like as an educational leitmotif. This psychical wandering begins with an introduction to his body, a portal to understanding the anxiously titillating excitement he experienced while riding horses or motorbikes, and the conflicted desire that surrounded it. He states, "Images of bikes and planes and horses merged for me, as did images of bikers and cowboys and pilots whom I imagined to be in precarious but jubilant control of their powerful mounts" (3). In his descriptions, Sacks is already alerting the reader to the conditions of his education; that is, peril was a predictable companion of certainty. This trope signals a kind of fragility lurking around his experience of schooling that will reemerge both for Sacks and for me in working through our education in a learning profession. In his opening memoir statements, Sacks also alludes to a somatic orientation to time, having to do with the body. For Sacks, the time before medical school started precisely with his body: movement before language, coupled with a longing for escape. A conflict and a body. If I wanted to read a bit further into it, perhaps the body was the conflict for Sacks. There is more to say about this specific interpretation later in his book. For me, the time before medical school was, similarly, a conflict about bodies. To be more precise, the time before medical school started with the uncomfortable dismembering of bodies.

Summers brought to me a welcome reprieve from long dusty bus rides on gravel roads to and from country school. The endless, stretched out moments of the prairie sky animated something that I now can understand as a contented loneliness. Our farm was hemmed in by foursquare country miles, big by local standards, boasting large herds of cattle and hogs as an income source, as well as numerous species of fowl intended for a Sunday dinner platter, and where horses, sheep, cats, and dogs were often christened with pet names. To cut costs, my dad would act in lieu of a veterinarian and perform minor surgeries, fill in as a birth attendant at the endless arrivals of mammalian newness, and regularly give needles brimming with pink medicines to alleviate suffering. He routinely stitched up lesions on hog bellies and in the cold of winter would sink his arm into the depths of a cow to pull out a calf.

My dad stitched animals together but he also cut them up. Butchering was a dreaded event that predictably interrupted my holiday reverie and brought all kinds of fantastic atrocities to our farm. Culturally, my parents embraced the value of producing their own food and sharing it with others. Neighbors and extended family would descend on our farm at sunrise, razor-sharp knives in hand, a tangible anticipation in the air, everyone eager to join in on the hanging evisceration of whatever was to be sacrificed for our tables. "Running like a chicken with your head cut off" was not a metaphor on our farm. It was a literal, grotesque event witnessed firsthand that required a child develop to survival tactics. To this day, the featherless chicken with its knurled, hanging skin and outstretched neck looking for its head still makes me uncomfortable.

The men who peeled back the hide of a cow with swift, skilled, pointed knife strokes would let me see what was actually skin deep. Butchering never lost its allure for me, gut-wrenching as it was. For example, some nerve fibers have, well, a lot of nerve. The segmented pieces of butchered meat lying on the table would twitch now and again. I recall standing and rubbing my eyes to see if I was imagining things and later asked my dad about it. For him there was no excitement in this surreal event; a gruff huff was mustered with no explanation of the spooky strangeness in front of me. And while I was fascinated, the horrors of these somatic experiences were not tamed over time. Being in the weird wake of having observed a live being, registering as something at once familiar and recognizable, undergo a careful stripping of itself until only a segmented skeleton remained, has stayed with me over time.

First Account: Show and Tell

I started medical school suspicious of the program's claims that student diversity in the form of different educational backgrounds would create a rich atmosphere of resources in which fellow learners would both appreciate and utilize the novelty inherent in the student constellation. I was grateful for the chance to belong where I suspected I did not. After completing two undergraduate music degrees, education had primarily been a focused foray into musical performance and I had become accustomed to arias, Brahms nocturnes, and *tempo rubato*. An interiority had been constructed over the years of stringent training as a vocalist and pianist that registered more as an opus of *sensing* than *knowing*. During my time studying music in university, I learned about a medical school accepting students with no formal science training. I wondered if the kind of sensing I had come to increasingly rely on in music could be transposed into an inclusive language reflective of a valuable interdisciplinary currency as an antidote to potential or perceived hard knowledge deficiencies. I had always been interested in what I understood medicine to be, and only ever imagined its defining possibilities as being a male in his early twenties who had excelled in the sciences. In my imagination, I was not eligible. I was a woman who had grown up in a small Mennonite prairie farming community with no female physicians to pique a possible career imaginary. I didn't have a science background, and at the time of application, I was in my late twenties and was convinced that there would be an suspension on applications from geriatric learners like me. My acceptance letter into medical school, however, suggested otherwise.

I read with anticipation how Sacks entered into professional learning as a neurology trainee. My own curriculum of anxiety and anxious logic as a psychiatry resident was palpable — a tender spot that I would iteratively return to, leading to a kind of chronic nervous condition, particularly as it relates to that mysterious moment where knowledge meets the demands of bedside caring. Sacks doesn't seem to be fussed about the start to his training, or maybe I misread his silence on the matter. His first account of postgraduate learning in neurology is a memory of journal clubs, a time for doctors in training to analyze research relevant to the care of patients. In my experience, journal clubs became a competition of critique where learners show their knowledge about research methodologies through scientific appraisal of the research study. The focus of these discussions would rarely move toward conversations of patient care and instead provided endless fodder for arguments about the perceived robustness of the study, leading me to the observation that it is the empiricism itself that was unconsciously venerated. Although Sacks's (2016) description of journal club is brief, I see many possible interpretations emerging from his encounter, where a great deal is happening despite the limited description. Sacks suggests to his UCLA learning cohort that in addition to poring over scientific journal articles hot off the press, they should also situate patient observations against nineteenth-century historical readings. He then goes on to point out, "They made little reference to anything more than five years old" (102). He laments that his proposition to read historical texts is discounted by his colleagues as archaic and obsolete. At this point in his memoir, the tone of his writing has an unusual bite in contrast to an otherwise gentle tone. He states, "It was as if neurology had no history" (102). Sacks suggests, even at this early stage of training, that the journal articles will fail them in their seeking to understanding what medicine is about.

On the heels of Sacks's truncated critique about the immaturity of information being used in medical training, my mind shifts to the imaginary of free association. I am caught by the link between Sacks's lack of confidence in empirical studies and his dismay about relying on research published in the past five years. The number five jumps out at me, and I am left thinking about Sacks and his colleagues as five-year-olds, animated in their classroom talk. But five-year-olds are typically in kindergarten, and kindergarten talk implies learning the ABC's. Similarly, in Sacks's description of his journal club event, grown-up language is temporarily kicked to the curb, and we read that Sacks can't really do anything as this drama unfolds. Sacks suggests, even at this early stage of training, that the journal articles will fail to help them in understanding what medicine is about. He too is left tongue-tied where the language required for reading research statistics and empirical findings is still nascent for Sacks. In my reading of Sacks's journal club, the scientific data his group attempts to access does not tell the full story. They, too, are working to master a language that will not be reliable for some time to come. For Sacks in this first recollection of medical learning, it is ironically the absence of reliable language insinuated in his journal club-turned-kindergarten that strikes me as inchoate. Sacks's narration of this embryonic event leads me to wonder about scenes of his childhood. What happened to Sacks as a boy?

As if Sacks (2016) can read my mind, he soon leads the reader to the scene of his boyhood, telling us, "As a chemistry-mad boy, I devoured books on the history of chemistry, the evolutions of its ideas, and the lives of my favorite chemists" (102). His childhood recollections offer something far richer and more sophisticated than the description of his journal club experience: words encountered as emotional alchemy spoken by authors whom he could look up to, presumably at a time when language itself was still emerging and during a time when he was at boarding school and his parents were absent. Sacks is onto something here; he offers us a scene of his natality and lets us know where he came from and what he longed for. The scenes of science are the images that will account for words when language will not do. It is almost as if Sacks's education speaks to a time when he is without language, or before language. This is not the only time Sacks will rely on images to speak for him.

Prior to starting his career as a staff neurologist, Sacks (2016) participated in a prestigious neurological exhibit and described himself in this academic encounter: "The exhibit was my way of introducing myself, saying, 'Here I am, look what I can do' to the neurological community in the States" (130). Through his writing about this encounter, Sacks again renders himself childlike. In imagining this adult turned childlike situation being further animated, I can almost hear his pleading tone at the neurology exhibit, calling out to his parent for undivided attention to be seen and to offer himself along with his academic interests as the object of show-and-tell. Through this encounter, another important moment has been written into Sacks's absence of words: in his professional academic debut, Sacks forgoes the opportunity to or give a traditional oral presentation. Data, graphs, median values, and other parameters that predictably insist on ancillary language to make meaning of science are not what Sacks chooses. Instead, he describes his public foray or "coming out" into academic medicine as an event at which he shows himself to his counterparts, without language, relying instead on the aesthetic of images. In his first scientific conference, Sacks presented photographs as a way of communicating. He gives the reader very little information about this encounter, simply stating that the photographic images of axonal dystrophies represented "special beauties and interests" (130) to him. The feminine qualities become the data that the reader registers. Intentionally or not, feminine qualities are associated with Sacks's introduction to academic medicine.

The image on Sacks's book cover also introduces him to readers and orients them prior to reading the title. On the cover, he sits, young, confidently straddling a motorbike, a body silhouette clad in jeans and leather, cut with delicate but substantive muscular precision. I was visually halted into thinking about why Sacks would begin his memoir with this image. Confidence, certainty, beauty, and an object of adoration can be read into the cover image, suggesting that this very image and its veracities will reappear in the pages to come. But I believe Sacks had something else in mind. After turning the last page of a beautifully articulated life journey deeply intertwined with medicine, it appears that the cover image speaks to Sacks's longings and how they figured into his search for understanding. It is the image of his desires that he uses to visually introduce himself, highlighting a tension about showing and telling in education.

Being at Odds, Arriving at a Who

An interesting educational marker therefore emerges in Sacks's descriptions. Showing who he was proved to be an important mode of communication in medicine, and putting himself on display allowed a showing of himself that was femininely oriented through the aesthetic of images, and paradoxically without language. This introduction to Sacks's medical education in neurology sets a collision course for the reader, signaling an important educational idea about the very idea of learning. That is, learning about who he is will be at odds with learning the demands of education. Throughout his time in medicine, Sacks is often in conflict with himself as he discovers educational coordinates set out to position him antagonistically with the course of recognizing who he is. What then, is he saying with this introduction of himself? Who is he as a neurologist is a question with pressing importance. It is the very question for him, as it is for all of us in medicine, to grapple with as we enter professional training. However, the *who* of us as physicians often gets confused with *what are we learning?* What can I read then from Sacks's rich, foreshadowing descriptions that hint at early beginnings of an education about who he is, without words?

The work of a memoir can be thought of as an autoethnographic encounter, where the self, through personal narrative, is the object under cultural investigation. Storytelling, narrative, and selfhood collide in a written effort to understand who someone uniquely is. Philosophy as the study of knowledge should offer something important in the discourse of self-knowledge and, in particular, about self-knowledge within an education of philosophy. Adriana Cavarero (2000) writes about self-representation as a genre that challenges the historical constitution of the philosophical subject and its analytical assumptions by insisting that the confines of philosophy collapse under the possibility of narrative. A who can be known, although not in an epistemological sense, but only through a narration of the person as protagonist in their own storied experience. Cavarero suggests that the *who* of an individual eludes philosophical knowledge in that the singularity of the individual demands an alternative to the language of the universal prevalent in philosophical discourse. This evasion can be seen as an intentional way of grappling with the confining phenomenology arriving at *what* something is. In other words, philosophy's main ambition has been to determine what a human is relative to other species.

A major focus of Hannah Arendt's (1958) writing concerns the philosophical aporia in considering the *who* and the *what*. She states, "The manifestation of who the speaker and doer unexchangeably is, though it is plainly visible, retains a curious intangibility that confounds all efforts toward unequivocal verbal expression. The moment we want to say who somebody is, our very vocabulary leads us astray into saying what he is" (181). Cavarero (2000) argues that beyond these distinctions, problematic fault lines emerge when it comes to knowing who someone is, fault lines that would find us reverting to discussions that deteriorate into notions of what a person is. To say more about how these cracks create problematic places for us in education leads to ontological orientations on the discourse of subject formation. The subject in education can be understood as play on words, where the self as a unique human being desires intelligibility, and at the same time, the subject in education can refer to a topical focus. For Arendt (1958), the intelligibility of an individual is made possible through narrative (50). Cavarero's conditions for intelligibility rely on the need for another. This relational condition for intelligibility is critical in constituting modes of communication, which for Cavarero (2000) is a mode that sidesteps subjectification in the ways that philosophy has insisted upon. Instead, Cavarero introduces a sayability that does not start with language but, rather, "he/she is a flesh and blood existent whose unique identity is revealed *ex post facto* through the word of his or her life story" (xiii).

Cavarero's writing here signals to me an opportunity to make a U-turn and revisit the notion of the body figuring into Sacks's first descriptions of his life story, albeit a body that, according to Cavarero, is not alone. Cavarero shapes my reading of Sacks in that his early introductions of himself as the subject in his memoir start with images acting as visual descriptions of himself encountered precisely because the reader is there to witness him. The offering of himself through his narrated body, or "flesh and blood existent," also enacts a beginning for he himself despite being a subject of medical education where intelligibility about Sacks or his story is often muddled. Yet Sacks is made coherent nonetheless because I, and others, have read him.

More fault lines emerge when comparing Sacks's writing of himself with the demands of training that require the skills of history taking. As I have said, history taking is a necessary element of every patient's encounter in which a story is told by the patient about the health problems they are experiencing, interpreted by the medical professional, and then entered into a patient chart, predictably in third-person account. There is an implicit understanding within the profession that the role of the physician's account is to offer expert objectivity within the subjective exchange and to translate the patient experience into a diagnostic possibility. Despite the richness that is available in eliciting patient stories, the narrative undergoes a process of retelling or medical filtering or retrofitting, where the bits that are not obviously relevant to the diagnosis are in fact the good bits that risk getting lost because they do not register as germane to the patient's story. In the physician's telling of the story, the patient is historically and culturally predetermined through a listening hypothesis and reliance on symptom pattern recognition in search of the diagnosis, ultimately leading to therapeutic treatment of the philosophical *what,* otherwise understood as the problem at hand. Here, the notion of the universal or the generalizable and not the who of the person is rendered desirable and useful in considering the patient. There is little room for a person's life specificity unless the patient's constellation and course of symptoms are so unrecognizable they register as a special "case study," a study worthy of publication precisely because its uniqueness could not be captured by expert knowledge. Beyond the latter situation, both writer and patient are philosophically constituted in the above interpellation, reduced to historical subjects without the potential of entering into a dramatic and potentially generative event afforded by narrative methodology.

Both the task of doing medicine and the act of being educated by medicine organize a kind of surgical undergoing as it relates to personal storytelling. In medicine, efficiency demands that we cut to the quick and arrive at an expert diagnosis. In doing so, excision of the *who* is at stake. In my experience, there is an unspoken rule in medicine that stories don't really matter. In fact, stories are perceived as an unreliable method of knowing. Yet Sacks's memoir demands a type of methodological reckoning not commonly offered nor frequently available within medical education, leaving him metaphorically speechless if he were to rely on the traditional writing conduits in medicine to tackle his personal historical narrative within medicine. According to Cavarero (2000), narration renders a unique fragility through the register of desire. She postulates that between narration and the notion of identity is a determined relation of desire, fundamentally defining the ineffable uniqueness of the person. What of desire in medicine and its education? Sacks's memoir tells us that the discourse of desire was frequently relegated to the contrary space of the secretive, the hidden, and the feminine. Sacks's writing may, in fact, be read as a literary act of resistance in response to an establishment in which he repeatedly felt on the outs. Alice Pitt (2003) describes this kind of resistance as curious in its consideration of "emancipatory hopes, where critical knowledge can be made from the refusal of official discourse" (47). Pitt's incisiveness gives way to a better understanding of how Sacks's memoir is an education of critical self-knowledge and a generative act of resistance to a presumed familiarity rendering him and his desires similar to others acting on the behalf of medicine.

Detached

But Sacks's story as a medical trainee is also one of not being comfortable in his own skin. Sacks admitted to a serious drug addiction throughout much of his formal neurology training in the 1960s that remarkably went largely undetected. The psychotic state induced by amphetamines would create a veil of detachment, from himself and the world around him, paradoxically probing prolific creativities foundational to his future medical genius. His drug use during neurology training seemed antiphonal in nature, a call to saturate the lonely ache of love unrequited, countered by formidable sympathomimetic pleasures. Sacks (2016) describes the experience as "mindless and all-sufficient — I needed nothing and nobody to 'complete' my pleasure — it was essentially complete, though completely empty. All other motives, goals, interests, desires, disappeared in the vacuousness of the ecstasy" (128). His admission of addiction stuns me. He was capable of managing specialty training in medicine while loosely tied to reality. He writes, "I would be back at work on Monday mornings — shaken and almost narcoleptic — no one, I think, realized that I had been in interstellar space, or reduced to an electrified rat, over the weekend" (129).

I am astonished by this account in thinking that no one, be it supervisors, teachers, nurses, fellow residents, medical students, or patients, presumably noticed. How could this be? If his shaken and narcoleptic self recovering from a weekend binge was in fact noticed by anyone, Sacks does not tell us. Alternatively, if noticed by his teachers, there would likely have been the question about what precisely to do. In my experience with medical education, physicians and their addictions are understood as an inevitable statistic, but nobody wants to be the human data that counts toward its epidemiology. Sacks was lucky. Or maybe I don't know what else to call it. In my encounters with this issue, suspicions of learner substance abuse is a messy business. I say this because the educational supervisor who raises the concern often becomes the concern when they shine light on a pattern of substance use meant to be hidden at all costs. Of course, the likelihood of medical trainees or physicians abusing substances is not insubstantial nor unfamiliar, and often takes on the form of a secretive and lonely journey. The question is, how far will the student go? In my experience as a medical educator, the labyrinthian processes that the supervisor and learner must go through, dubiously masked as *providing support* to the supervisor and learner alike, is fatiguing to write about. Of course, patient safety is a priority, but typically it is not the safety of patient care that first registers as a problematic sign. The outcome of this fraught process is typically a seriously fractured relationship between learner and teacher. Not because it has to be that way but because relational skills seem limited in dealing with this chasm. So medical education can be something that must be endured, predicated on a belief that at a very basic level, time multiplied by experience — even if this includes an unacknowledged addiction — makes physicians of us all.

However, this myth of endurance is turned upside down for Sacks. He has seemingly been absent during his time as a neurology resident and yet was sufficiently present in his distracted experience to satisfy the rubric of the day. A kind of fatalistic bravery in defying an academic institution historically made from medical expertise draws me into the moment that Sacks offers, or, perhaps more specifically, what he omits. From my reading of Sacks, his supervisors did not, could not, or would not engage the chaos that plagued him. Perhaps this deliberate turning away registered as an educational disregard for Sacks, setting up a kind of polarity within his education where he was both at odds with this education and simultaneously the odd man out. I sense that Sacks too felt deeply out of place, and his resistance to being present speaks to an education nonadherent to classic metrics of success, suspended in time. This type of temporal suspension may have simultaneously created a demand to be noticed and a demand for a wordless space for the working out of an emotional logic that would find itself using the educational stage as a personal encounter.

Sacks (2016) writes about perceptions of himself as an "embarrassment" to the neurology department but stated that his successful publications saved him such that he was also seen as an "ornament" (122). I wonder whose perspective he is taking when he writes this criticism, including the temporality he has in mind when he sees himself as painfully inadequate. Is he writing about the young adult Sacks or a version of himself that is much more childlike? This brief, vulnerable sentence is situated within descriptions of his medical education and says far more about what is not being said. Threat is readily implied within his education. He is repeatedly toying with death through his intense drug addiction and learning a profession of caring at the same time. More accurately, in returning to the work of Cavarero, we are encountering a working out of who Sacks is which his who-ness is now in relationship with his education. We may, albeit inaccurately, come to the premature conclusion that Sacks is a drug addict. This is the *what* of philosophy that limits an understanding of the uniqueness and ineffability of what is at play for Sacks as the protagonist of his story. There is something far more generative occurring in his subsequent description of himself during this part of his education that is valiant in its approach. Danger is lurking such that Sacks's account of playing with death can be read as a kind of attempt at learning what he is resistant to and writing his way out of a complete disaster by speaking the unspoken. Recognizing what is at stake, Sacks speaks to himself in a pointed, no-nonsense manner saying, "Oliver, you will not see another New Year's Day unless you get help. There has to be some intervention" (144). Thematics of death now begin to figure concretely into his memoir. This will be the start of a series of mistakes that he writes freely about in publishing a pedagogy of failure on the part of his teachers, and that also acts, in part and paradoxically, as "the help" in his medical education.

Early in his training, Sacks describes the case of a patient whom he finds endlessly interesting in the patient's enigmatic failure to fit classical diagnoses. Sacks (2016) writes that his curiosity led him to think, "What's going on inside there? I wish I could *see* your brain" (105). Sacks's desire to penetrate the skull was fulfilled. Shortly after leaving his clinic, the patient was struck by a truck in a fluke encounter and died instantly, leaving Sacks with the patient's post-mortem brain in his hands. Sacks reflects, "Could my wish to see his brain have played a part in his fatal accident? I could not help wondering too, whether he had decided to end things and stepped deliberately in front of the truck" (105). Sacks's imaginary, including omnipotently murderous whimsies, is offered up like an earnest child with a nescient confession. Or perhaps this is how I imagine Sacks narrating a sentiment where he has lost sense of what is really happening. Scenes of death continue in his memoir, albeit, I suspect, with a black humor at play.

As a bench scientist with dreams of success, Sacks (2016) is tasked with meticulously dissecting myelin from thousands of earthworms in an attempt to study invertebrate nerve conduction. He also admits to having an incredible fondness for cephalopods, a species without a skeleton that are almost phantomlike in their ability to hang together. And so, his dissection of these species-as-friends is a murderous act he engages in for the sake of learning: "I committed a veritable genocide of earthworms in the college garden; thousands of earthworms would be needed to extract a respectable sample of myelin" (135–136). Sacks systematically articulates his failure in his research efforts gone disastrously wrong, describing how he first loses his written data strapped to his bike, then gets breadcrumbs into one of the centrifuge instruments meant to refine the myelin sample, and, finally, loses all his myelin data samples. The discovery of his fantastic successive failures prompts the following directive from his supervisors: "Sacks, you are a menace in the lab. Why don't you go and see patients — you'll do less harm" (137). In the wake of losing several months' worth of meticulously harvested data, Sacks is relegated to the clinical work of patient encounters, as though the work of humanity was less vulnerable, and second-rate in its nonresearch focus. And it is this very relegation that acts as an educational pivot in this poignant story. Sacks stumbles into the generative effect of loss. Who he is becomes narrated by a script in which he is protagonist, antagonist, and comic relief. And his story of failure points me to an educational moment that I avoided with all my heart and soul — that is, my own sense of being a who resisting the story of being anything less than an expert.

Sensing as Knowing

Self-directed learning was the pedagogical promise and curse embedded in the model of education adopted by the medical school I attended. We were assured that, as adults, we were in charge of our own learning and were encouraged to build on personal experiences, knowledge, and skills to meet program requirements. By the time I started medical school, I had become familiar with a world of employment and professional expectations making it relatively easy for me to speak with patients and to listen for stories, told and untold. Chairs pulled tightly against crammed-in hospital beds, a curtained veil of privacy pretending to seclude, I leaned in to hear past the delirious sounds of the hospital. Dreams and desires were really being spoken about, but it was easier to feign deafness, as there were few places for the wishes and the wants of patients to be truly heard unless they serendipitously corresponded to treatment protocols. My leaning toward a kind of sensing seemed to be helpful during patient encounters. However, I soon found out this was not as valuable a skill as I believed it to be.

The "real skills" had to do with human deconstruction, a taxonomized segmenting of the patient into granular symptoms, masticated until they were palatable to the profession, which often translated into lengthy discussions locating pathology or pathophysiology and then reciting evidence-based treatments indicated for each corresponding illness. I recall many bedside situations, learners like me wearing white coats, trying hard to play the part and yet not knowing our script nor the plot that would take us to the ending, talking about the patient who lay below, looking up at us. The consultant physicians would direct the unfolding drama. Questions were posed using terminology mostly understood by us but sufficient to register as clear anxiety. Our apportioned answers were often unsatisfactory, to my mind, but I found that I couldn't think beyond the encounter. The physicality of our positions around the bed foreclosed on a foreboding architecture that over time would be readily assumed by me — power and authority unquestioned and unchallenged. It registered initially as uncomfortable in its functional inevitability, yet over time I grew accustomed to it as an invisible cloak of confidence, defending against the ineptitude that taunted me.

Pharmakon

Only time would attend to this conflict in which language in medicine was like Derrida's *pharmakon* (Derrida and Johnson 1981, 70) in that it was both my illness and my cure. Initial conversations about training backgrounds were points of interest. Our medical student class had clergy, lawyers, musicians, dancers, scientists, and philosophers, to name a few. As medical training progressed, I sensed shifts in the dynamic of group learning where referring to your background was at times conflated with who would be legitimate when speaking about "real medicine." In this regard, my training in music was nice to have as a resource but not necessary when speaking about issues such as pathophysiology. And so I had to sound convincing, even if I wasn't. I learned how to leverage language as a way of defending against an identity that I felt I should dislike yet didn't. Although I felt I was frequently detached from knowledge that I should possess, I could string together language that cohered in the way that a good melody does. In doing so, I could survive the student competition in the program's pass/fail rubric by creating word aesthetics that sounded medically plausible in a commonplace vernacular frequently reduced to perfunctory utterances.

It is within this uncertainty that I stumbled into an unspoken, messy business of death that would transform into a kind of moral injury for me. In my senior year of medical training, I was on call on a general internal medicine ward and was paged at around 3 a.m. to a patient whose blood pressure was concerning to the nurse. The fact that the nurse was calling the medical student signaled to me that this was not a critically serious problem, but it was enough to incite my anxiety. These kinds of calls were given to medical students to help them think through potential causes prior to calling the senior resident, who would then review the case and intervene with some level of confidence and skill. While I knew that falling blood pressure could be a critical event, I reassured myself that an emergency such as this was far more likely to be recognized by the nurses and that the nurse would clearly know what to do. In other words, I tried to convince myself that I would not be needed to respond to a crisis, because if I were, I was convinced I would be unreliable as a resource to myself and others. I spoke briefly to the nurse, who indicated that the maximum amount of fluids had already been pumped into the intravenous line and now the question remained as to what to do next. She added, "It's a bit complicated."

I headed in to see the patient and found an enormous, naked, unrecognizable shape on the bed. The patient's kidneys had failed, leaving her incapable of processing her body chemistry; the net effect was an exogenous river of fluid finding its way into spaces not usually inhabited by water. Profound swelling engulfed her anatomy, leaving her skin literally splitting and weeping. I had seen bloated dead animals on the farm where I grew up and was no stranger to anatomical aberrations, nor to the grotesque. But this caught me off guard in a way that found me grateful that the patient was unconscious and therefore unable to register my reaction. Learning the technical term for her condition, "anasarca," offered a sterilized moniker. After speaking to the senior resident, who had nothing to add and likely as fearful of being chastised as I was, I called the on-call physician. Despite my trepidation, I was also angry at what I perceived to be an injustice to human dignity and wanted to understand the insanity I felt. The on-call physician sounded defeated. "Give her more fluid," he said.

I spit out the words, "She's dying."

"We haven't been able to reach the family to do anything else," he said. And I hung up the phone to share the instructions with the nurse. A suffocating sense of futility saturated me. Why couldn't death stitch up the patient's seeping wounds? Better yet, why couldn't death spray out her excess fluid in a grand, derisive cascade that would rain over my fearful confusion? The truth is, I was angry at how thin-skinned the patient was. Her friable dermis made the living barrier between us deeply uncomfortable. The patient's death would have made it much easier for me, creating an end point, instead of insisting on the next step, which was to tolerate a life that had no option other than to weep with iatrogenic tears, tears made from intravenous fluids for which I had now served as a partial conduit. While this fantasy was situated within a deep justified anger about an inoculation I had not seen coming, it also opened onto to another conflict. I could not authentically wear the sanctimony to which I had bound myself.

Penumbra of Confusion

An anxious logic clearly emerges for me in writing about writing. My thinking about dealing with the volume-overloaded patient was organized not only by anxiety but also by anger toward the patient whose condition, in my mind, had now been conflated with the human who suffered from it. And behind the fear was a deep worry that my presence somehow had an etiological effect on the suffering I saw. These thought processes justified a hostile resentment as a dynamic response to an inert situation that would take captive any meaningful response on my part other than to be in it. These conditions were not so dissimilar to the conditions of the patient lying in front of me. Wilfred Bion (1970) defines experience as frustration. He thinks of learning as getting to know emotional life where it has an unknowable quality to it that must be endured. Bion's "negative capability" refers to the ability to stay with and tolerate the frustrating conditions of uncertainty, a place that has to do with not reaching for quick solutions but instead getting to know frustration as experience. My desire to escape the learning experience of unknowability was something that I repeatedly fantasized about in a career oriented toward understanding and answering though understanding is often simply not possible. Unknowability is a place of frailty that I would frequently inhabit and return to, while simultaneously wanting to run from and never return. Helplessness was a costume that was not comfortably worn when the script called for confidence and expertise. But the reflexivity of the moment, I thought, called for escape from the moment. Bion sees it otherwise and suggests that experience as a learning construct is about leaning into the challenge of knowing emotional life and remaining present within the penumbra of confusion. Here, quick fixes and easy outs do not mend the learning pain. Instead, learning calls for a steady warming to doubtful uncertainty as a way of creating emotional clarity.

Turning back to Sacks, the subjective observations he offers about his education and the various ways in which he works with the conflicts he encounters very much act as exemplars of Keats's (1988) "negative capability" (539). Sacks doesn't really talk about his "education" per se, in that he is not regurgitating knowledge and facts acquired within a clinical or research curricula. Rather he is telling his life story about who he is, in a roundabout manner, or, at times, being completely uncertain about where things are headed. His narrative is similar to other medical memoirs that I have read in that it is not specifically nor exclusively the classroom encounter that is recalled as education — it is everything that surrounds it, making life the classroom in which he is learning and the one worth narrating. Sacks's story is one of changing his mind in his attempts at understanding his own emotional life, which at first appears to be increasingly inaccessible to him. It is this place of suspension and emotional chasm that resonates as a different kind of education.

Going Too Far

In thinking about education, Deborah Britzman (2009) writes, "It is as if the very thought of education will never let us go beyond what has already happened and so refuses to grow up" (1). Britzman is speaking to a past that not only intrudes on the present but also highlights a problematic about emotional life that does not pay any heed to our attempts at suppressing uncomfortable memories or forgetting. In doing so, the past inconveniently taps us on the shoulder, asking us to return to what has not yet been resolved. This call to return to the past reminds me of an experience in the early days of medical school in which one of our introductory lectures focused on learning about ethics and our responsibility to the public. The lecture hall was crammed with young adults, yet-to-be doctors, presumably too naive or too successful to understand the dangers that lie within us, and listening to a lecture that seemed mostly irrelevant. Most of us likely had not had enough lived history as physicians to situate the seriousness of the discussion. The topic turned to the issue of personal boundaries. The presenter spoke with a kind of evangelical fervor that made me wonder what had happened in her past to create such insistence. The lecturer issued a strong advisement against touching patients outside of the physical exam encounter, as touch could be considered a violation of trust in a dynamic already marked by inequities of power and position. While it may be clear to us what our intent was in touching patients, the risk would manifest in the patient's interpretation. Furthermore, she advised that we should not be on a first name basis with our patients. Patients are not friends. We ought to refer to them by their christened or preferred names, however they should not refer to us by our first names without the title of "Dr." to keep everyone oriented to the relationship at hand.

Looking back, I can now put words to the educational dilemma that was unfolding in front of me. I understood the delicate need for awareness, caution, good judgment, and a commitment to patient safety. However, what was felt at the time of this encounter has become an emotional blueprint guiding a de facto response within me, rightly or wrongly. The patient, in this teaching encounter, was situated as the wild card, with a not-so-subtle hinting at an unpredictable, dangerous subjectivity at hand. While the presenter stopped short of saying this, the emotional register of it shouted at us: How do you help someone who is dangerous to you? How could I stay within the lines when I was being told that the patient would not?

I was just beginning to locate the deep discomfort inside me, although my friend, seated next to me, beat me to it. "Harms," she said, "We're fucked. People don't follow these kinds of rules. And most of the time, we don't follow these rules either."

The truth was, I was rattled. How would I know when I was relationally safe with my patients? Did our medical teachers really see us as responses to unwieldy libidos that would overtake better judgment? The learning situation I had just encountered spoke to the delusional belief that culture, and particularly medical culture, could be managed in a way that assured safety. But how could I know if I had gone too far? I wasn't talking about abuse or egregious aggression. I was talking about daily relational encounters that were being sterilized for the sake of an academic discussion. Yet such discussions did not begin to acknowledge the dangers at play where emotions were present, which, incidentally, is everywhere.

My friend was righter than I could have ever imagined. People don't follow the rules that medicine sets out. Early on in my child and adolescent psychiatry career, I had the privilege of working with homeless and street involved youth. I really had no idea what it was like to live on the streets, and so I had to rely on stories told by my patients that would feed my own imaginary. I worked closely with an adolescent youth whose life had been cut to the quick by experiences with poverty, racialization, discrimination, mental illness, and a net effect of feeling as though her very presence was an insult to the space she inhabited. Her mother's fatal drug overdose became a frequent point of conversation for us. For years, my patient struggled intensely with dizzying self-harm, repeated suicide attempts, high-risk behaviors, and dangerous drug use. She was typically quiet, soft-spoken, thoughtful, and intensely perceptive. She also had zero regard for what most people had to say and knew that her life was not like other lives. Yet she never missed appointments with me. At the end of one of our last sessions, in which we had negotiated her "safety" for the next week, she got up to leave and ambled to the door. She turned around and said, "Dr. H, can I tell you something?"

"Of course," I said.

She hesitated and then said, "You are the closest thing to a mother I have ever had. I love you."

I too had come to care deeply about her in a way that I am sure many professionals care about their patients. Did I love her? With what I knew of the different kinds of love that we can have for our friends, our community, our earth — the answer was a definitive yes. But I wasn't experienced enough to trust that I was not the only one who had ever held intense emotions for patients without it somehow being wrong, especially the kind of affective pull for this brittle youth whose life always hung in the balance. Still, in the vulnerable moment of her confession, the voice of the lecturer screamed in my head, demanding neutrality, an emotional tabula rasa that would respond without a reciprocal confession of love. My position of power and a statement of affect would surely make its intent ugly. I was flattened in this moment and hoped that my pained expression would convey the deep caring I felt for her. I think I said something like "You too are deeply loved by many people."

Her limp body was found hanging from a park swing set a short time later.

The discursive act of writing about this intensely painful experience provides a kind of retrospective clarity that was not afforded in those conflicted moments. The temporality of coming to this experience is misleading, as I am returning to what has already happened, which, at the time of the event, I could not have known. In the act of writing, I am attributing emotional experiences to a memory, as opposed to the event itself. The event has passed but still holds an emotional valence for me, one that keeps working itself through over time.

Nachträglichkeit is a term Freud coined to understand temporal and typically traumatic connections within the psychical workings of the mind where recall is imbued with assigned significance and not necessarily preoccupied with the memory itself (Eickhoff 2006). On the topic of *Nachträglichkeit*, Pitt (2003) says, "Traumatic experience creates a tear in our very capacity to make sense of the event, indeed, to fully experience the event. At the same time, we are drawn to the hole, compelled by some force to worry about it" (96). It is easy to imagine then my own ripped capacity riddled by dread, fear, emptiness, and hollow despair following my adolescent patient's death. The enormity of the loss saw my own professional pettiness rear its ugly head in the perseverating about how she should be remembered, who should be present to do so, and what hospital rules applied for those healthcare workers who wanted to attend her funeral. I was spinning ungracefully and it was likely obvious to others that the ends of my professional self were seriously frayed in the wake of her violent departure, relegating me to anemic attempts at understanding what could not be known. In fact, in looking back, it was only ever possible to act before I knew what was really happening and to experience before I understood what was needed. I told myself repeatedly that I had not failed her and that I had done everything humanly possible and that her death would not become a fatal trademark for me as a child and adolescent psychiatrist.

As I lay in my partner's arms, someone who had worked as a teacher in youth corrections for decades and who was also no stranger to trauma, he told me, "Not all young people were meant to live."

It was a simple statement, which I initially registered as a kind of horrible, raw economy about human life that seemed impossible to accept. While his words were meant to provide an antidote to the crush of guilt that pressed upon me and help me move on, I found myself regressed and inhabiting a childlike version of myself I could not seem to shake. I could not see that I had also lost the capacity of my adult self, and had unknowingly returned to my own childhood, where another economy about life was pressed upon me.

As I mentioned in the first chapter, my father was a farmer who cared for many different kinds of animals. As a typical part of our world, dad would frequently load up dead animal carcasses on the front bucket of his tractor and drive them to a place in our back farm pasture that we referred to as the *pile of deads*. The animals on this pile were the ones whose lives were cut short because they were misfits or ill. They were the ones that couldn't make it, couldn't take it, or were never meant to be. Their lives marked a failure on the farm, specifically because they were of no use in that they could not be sold, nor butchered, nor were they worth the cost of the feed to keep them alive. But why? Dying was an everyday event. The loss of animal life was sad to be sure, but not unusual nor abnormal. So what was it about these lifeless animals hanging off the edge of the tractor that filled me with a creepy sense of hollowness?

I would sit perched on the edge of the tractor seat occupied by my dad, pressed up beside him and feeling safe within his large physical presence, open to the air, with the tractor motor deafening the possibility of conversation. Sometimes I would be given the delightful responsibility of guiding the big round steering wheel, replete with the belief that I was in control of where we were headed. But when we arrived at the pile to discard our load, my reverie would be interrupted by sightlines never meant to be seen. Hooves seemingly everywhere, milky eyes, tongues lolling sideways, and bloated bellies constituting a morphology registering as outright horror. The view of the pile pressed on me and seemed to obstruct my vision, no matter where I turned. I would be filled with an incredible sense of despondent sadness, even though I knew that the pile of deads existed.

I see now that the story of the pile of deads had come to comment on my reaction to my patient's death. I desperately wanted to create a safe place for my patient but was unsure if I could. Instead, the scene had turned Kafkaesque, in both my childhood and with my patient. Her death was a nightmare to me and had me returning to the lecture on boundaries. I didn't have to ask if my patient had gone too far. She clearly had. Was the lecturer correct about patients being dangerous, resonating as an eerie kind of prophesy? Was I culpable in her death because I had failed to see her potential to die? Did my patient's death mean that I too should be discarded onto a symbolic heap of useless clinicians? I found it hard to separate my patient from myself, leading to a deeply challenging time in my professional work.

It was no wonder than that the emotional residue following her death took the form of a kind of obsessional practice for me that could not tolerate errors. I would rehearse the aspects of her care in my head repeatedly until I had convinced myself that everything had been done. And then I would repeat this very ritual in an attempt to soothe what would not be soothed. I had entered into the tragedy of a tragic profession where the human must die, and I now understood this for my patient and for myself. In my mind, the very thought of errors in situations of care were too literally fatalistic until I could work through and understand the educational forces that refused symbolization of this unthinkable idea.

Implicit in this description of repeating and working through, and perhaps illustrative of it, is the idea that knowledge has its own unconscious life (Felman 1993). In my situation, a daily repetitive psychiatric practice of perfectionism intended to keep pain at bay would emerge as a form of negation against the pain of my patient's death and my own past. The barely tolerable fragments constituting the memory of my patient, my failed work, and my own worries about being discarded would break into my thought life, interrupting my clinical routines, and be insistent enough to resist any personal amnesty. The well-intentioned rule book offered to me as a medical student relying on a set of ethical commitments intended to create interpersonal boundaries as a practice point of clarity was read by me as irrelevant in an emotional collision course with another path that would be forged in a temporality I came to refer to as the time of after. My patient's death was paradoxically an unwelcome beginning where I would find myself encountering a learning constituted by a need for a kind of public evacuation of self under an untenable situation of ethics gone wild. I needed to seek shelter and hide for self-preservation. I was being forced to reckon with my own past in order to come to some kind of reckoning with medicine. I needed to grow up, psychodynamically speaking, by stitching together my memory of painful events with the emotions of the memory, which up until now had been separate encounters. Perhaps this is what drew me to Sacks, as he too would encounter traumatic collisions in his learning made from the residue of history, simultaneously creating a demand to go underground as a way of both tolerating the present and reckoning with the past, and emerging as a whole person.

Sex and Medicine

The heaviness of death in the work of medicine often requires a reprieve, which can take many forms. Despite the many challenging encounters Sacks had in medicine, he also describes playful encounters, albeit with unlikely friends. His motorbike, as I said earlier, is symbolically and literally important in his education. It is his earliest companion, his playmate introduced on the very first page of his memoir and featured on the book cover. It is as though his motorbike has always existed, present in anticipation of his story and ready to take him away from his story as needed. Before there is medicine, there is his escape. Sacks (2016) describes his bike with an emotional longing so delicate and poignant, the reader wonders what or who he is really writing about. He says, "There is a direct union of oneself with a motorcycle, for it is so geared to one's proprioception, one's movements and postures, that it responds almost like part of one's own body. Bike and rider become a single, indivisible entity" (97). The rider and the ridden are one. Suddenly, play takes on sexual overtones, and this deeply intimate description blushes with suggestion, adolescent idealism, and carnal fascination. But what of this kind of play in Sacks's medical education? Or rather, what of these adolescent longings or fantasies in medicine? The reader is caught off guard and we feel as though we have stumbled into Sacks's personal diary instead of his memoir about becoming a neurologist. Reading his text closely, I have to wonder what is happening. Is he talking about life? Or education, sex, and medicine? And can these be thought of as a singular idea?

Later in his book, Sacks (2016) refers to a few lines from Thom Gunn's "The Allegory of the Wolf Boy," a poem that plays with the overlap of seeming contradictions:

> At tennis and at tea
> Upon the gentle lawn, he is not ours
> But plays us in a sad duplicity

Sacks writes with an incisive clairvoyance, capturing the heart of the matter by saying, "This corresponded to a certain duplicity I felt in myself, which I thought of in part as a need to have different selves for day and night. By day I would be the genial, white-coated Dr. Oliver Sacks, but at nightfall I would exchange my white coat for my motorbike leathers and, anonymous, wolf-like, slip out of the hospital to rove the streets" (78). He was twenty-seven at the time and his coming out registered as multiple duplicities within himself later understood as intense shyness and a sexual orientation he was not yet comfortable with. His admission would have us ask what of the play that is at hand for Sacks? What does his sexuality have to do with medicine? Sacks is working through his own understanding of his sexuality while he is in medicine, and his writing gives us clues as to how the limits of medicine also constituted sexual limits for him. I find that his writing signals a deep tension between his experience of his public self and that of his private self. In acknowledging this strain, he invites the reader to enter into personal, sexual spaces not typically meant to be curricular in medicine. However, his writing is courageous in his suggestion that he also experienced sexual longings in the medical classroom that were perhaps uninvited and awkward but present nonetheless. He first communicates this untold tale by way of another story.

Sacks tells us that when he turned forty he had an unexpected birthday present: he is groped by a stranger in the water while he goes for a swim. The stranger invites him to have sex, and they do. Sacks (2016) tells us, "It was just as well that I had no foreknowledge of the future, for after that sweet birthday fling I was to have no sex for the next thirty-five years" (203). Sacks returns to this ingress a second time in his book by recalling a time during an interview for a position at a hospital when he blurts out that he has not had sex for thirty-five years in response to a question asking for his social insurance number. And he gets more intimate. In another segment of his memoir, Sacks brings us into his bedroom and permits us to be voyeurs in his intensely detailed description of a particular sexual encounter with a roommate who he found attractive. He describes ejaculating while he is giving his roommate a massage, which was responded to with silence and harsh rejection. As Sacks laments the pain of going too far, he is reminded that his lover's name is the same as the initials for his mother.

As I read this, I almost laughed at the Freudian delight of it all but also felt deeply pained at the dismissals constituting Sacks's experiences. In what feels like peering over the centerfold of a tabloid publication with Sacks as the model, we get a sneak peak into Sacks's private life while simultaneously reminding ourselves that we are in medical school and ought to be looking at human anatomy and its functions only for anatomy's sake. But then he turns the page for us and offers raw images of adolescent homosexual desires come true, replete with titillating details about unrequited sexual love in which his mother, of all people, is symbolically present. The seriousness returns quickly when thinking about the reality of Sacks as a gay, Jewish, British man after World War II. There were reasons to be quietly awkward, particularly in a medical culture venerating a phenotype of males that did not include Sacks. Within the story Sacks tells us there is an adolescent conflict and ideality working itself out through a psychoanalytic narrative of a gay man in a medical closet that is otherwise intended to tell us about his education, his relationship to his education, and his educational contributions as a physician.

What then is the nature of the homosexual closet in medical education? Mark Blechner's (2005) writing about the famous American psychiatrist and psychoanalyst Harry Stack Sullivan gives us some clues. Sullivan primarily practiced psychiatry in the 1920s and 1930s — a time where there were serious personal risks associated with being out, including incarceration. When Blechner reportedly suggested to a senior analyst that Sullivan was gay, assuming that this was an uncontested fact, he was met with defensiveness and challenge. Blechner writes, "It was an example of the fog of distraction, avoidance, and dissociation that has surrounded Sullivan's homosexuality" (1). But what is it about the bedroom antics now being spoken about in medicine that can be tolerated only through the fantastical imaginary or a resisting silence on the matter? Why is it that Sullivan and others associated with a gay orientation conjure up anticipatory dread when what happens in the bedroom should clearly take a back seat for any physician whose central task is the suffering patient — even if the suffering has to do with bedroom antics? This very question speaks to the conditions of the closet. It's not like there is an actual closet to look at, that is, a structure that will contain and hide whatever it is that becomes frightening and threatening to other physicians. But there is a body, and the body of the gay physician is what can be located and identified as the unsightly closet contents. Blechner insinuates that the very wondering then about whether or not the physician body participates in homosexual acts is sufficient to render diagnostics such as "schizoid or simply mysterious" (2), thereby enacting homophobia now translated within medicine into language of pathology or fantasy. Using this kind of language as a touchstone, medicine is weaponized against the gay physician whose body is the site of aberration, inevitably threatening a career's viability, or through willful blindness the gay physician is relegated to a peripheral place. The nature of the medical closet would inadvertently reinforce as intensely oppressive an existence for Sullivan as it did for Sacks, leaving him to contend with this deeply problematic conflation of heterosexual fears gone wild.

Blechner (2005) also noted that Sullivan's homosexuality was absolutely essential and integral to innovations in both his clinical and theoretical work. Blechner states, "Because there has been so much anxiety and mystification about his [Sullivan] homosexuality, the importance of his sexuality to his history has also been obscured" (3–4). The same argument can be made for Sacks but oriented toward reading his life as an educational narrative informed by psychoanalysis. It can be presumed that there is a dizzying confusion for Sacks when playing hide and seek in medicine. He comes out of the closet and then retreats into hidden, unspoken places. But there is no actual game at play. Homosexuality, from the nuanced written accounts of Sacks, had no place in medicine, forcing a decision algorithm for him in lieu of a risk assessment. What was at stake? What to do?

Sullivan reportedly opened a ward exclusively for gay young men diagnosed with Schizophrenia in the 1920s with an astonishing recovery rate for individuals with schizophrenia, despite the reality that Sullivan's interventions predated the advent of antipsychotic medications, which are currently thought of as the gold standard for the treatment of psychosis (Blechner 2005). In Sullivan's wards, biological recovery was clearly linked to cultural and interpersonal interventions, and a hospital atmosphere was created in which descriptions of sexual encounters by staff members were encouraged in order to reduce any closeted anxiety or stigma for the patients. This permission to verbally normalize homosexuality and simultaneously depersonalize the self from the pathological may have been what Blechner referred to when he described Sullivan as having an uncanny ability to connect with those who appeared disconnected, pointing out, "When he spoke with schizophrenics, they no longer sounded schizophrenic" (4). Sullivan's brilliance in understanding the poignant and deeply relational interface between health, mental life, and sexuality was ahead of his time.

Sacks too is talking about sexual exploration and sexual intimacy in his memoir, but something about it feels out of place, like he is telling us awkward secrets about his sexual life that are relegated to the status of too much information. My gut reaction, otherwise understood as a transference response, signals an opportunity to stop and pause. What is it about Sacks's telling that feels like he has gone too far? It is not the sexual details nor the image of sweaty bodies. Rather, it is the precarious vulnerability of making the gay bedroom a viable classroom in the recollection of his medical education. I wonder if Sacks felt as though the medical closet was a deep professional vice. Any type of coming out would certainly put Sacks deeply at odds with the unwieldy systemic oppression relying on polarizing attitudes, attitudes that insisted on conceptions of sexual orientation during Sacks's time as "normal" and "abnormal." My hesitation is read as a sense of dread for Sacks, but not dread about the commonplace experience of sexual encounters turned into the stuff of comedy, pain, or satisfaction. Rather, I dread the inevitable uncertain, paralyzing isolation inherent in attempting to break through the cemented stoicism pervasive in medical discourse that does not lean far from the axis of the heteronormative. An education about the healing of a body and mind was not offered to Sacks, just as his own suffering was not noticed, as far as we can tell. This kind of educational experience as an effect of his education is a prescription for the practice of caring he was to encounter. No wonder he gets stuck.

While Sacks's (2016) writing suggests that he is thinking in Sullivan's protesting footsteps, something is different for Sacks. Sullivan takes charge and builds a ward where he is in control of evoking a normalizing discourse about being gay for oppressed patients. In Sacks's recollections, he symbolically becomes the patient described in Sullivan's account, a patient in need of a normalizing discourse in a place where the silent opposition about his sexuality translates as the psychopathologizing homophobia that forms the bricks and mortar propping up the meaning of his medical school education. Sacks's mother, who is also a respected physician in his community, says to him after finding out that he is gay, "You are an abomination. I wish you had never been born" (9–10). Blechner's (2005) description of the plight of gay male patients is at the heart of the matter for Sullivan and Sacks. Blechner writes,

> In fact, one important source of his [Sullivan's] understanding of the embeddedness of psychopathology in interpersonal relations was his own experience of his homosexuality. Many a gay

man has tried to understand his experience of homosexuality intrapsychically, without reference to how it affects his relations with other people, and how his relations with other people affect his experience of his sexuality. You can scour your oedipal complex and preoedipal relations all you want, but if you don't take account of the fact that other people, shaped by social convention, are condemning you for an essential aspect of your being, you will never get anywhere. Sullivan recognized this. It was the insight behind his ward for gay schizophrenic men. (7)

The residue of this impossible situation constituted a relational positioning for Sacks in which he iteratively returned to longing for inclusivity in his writing, a perspective that was on the outs in a medical world dominated by heteronormativity. His sexual exclusion would seep into his academic encounters, challenging the idea that sex or sexuality is only for the bedroom. And for Sacks, an important orientation to belonging and being accepted in an academic environment where, unlike most of his colleagues, he was ostracized, was to identify a space that would allow for deep interrogations into himself as a gay man, writer, and artist working in the field of medicine. Sacks (2016) says, "I did have a position. At the heart of medicine. That's where I am" (222). Recalling Cavarero, he might well have said, "This is *who* I am."

Three

A Psychiatrist's Body

Sacks's experience with the medical closet and his longing for inclusivity signals a duplicitous tension, symbolically existing within his own body. While his body was a medical body needed to heal others and prop up the work of neurology, his physical body, capable of desire, simultaneously rendered him excluded. His conflicted experience of medicine enacting a type of biological warfare directed at what his body represented would have me ask the same question about my experience as a woman in academic psychiatry. As with Sacks, spaces of dismissal in medicine were often too close for comfort for me. Without really being able to articulate it at the time, this looming sense of personal exclusion constituted an odd liminal geography mapping onto the perpetual uncertainty described by Wilfred Bion, while at the same time I was heavily relied upon to be present for the day-to-day clinical work of psychiatry. I will describe this no-woman's-land more specifically later in this chapter, but I am struck by the question of how I might understand this kind of gendered judgment constituting a form of silent governance shaping my mind and directing my body. More specifically, I have been pressed to grapple with finding a way out of this not-so-clandestine curriculum, but could only begin to do so through struggling with the educational meaning of it all. Deborah Britzman's (2021) formulation of education, paraphrased, suggests that education is not just what happens to us but rather is the meaning that we make of what has already happened to us. I too had to make meaning of my body in psychiatry through a search for my own voice specifically as a representation of my body, which was slow to be heard, although present nonetheless.

While it is clear that bodies matter in medicine, I want to consider three intertwining problems when thinking about what bodies are for in psychiatry: judgment, authority, and relationality. It is not difficult to imagine how judgment is often conflated with authority in medicine and vice versa, pointing to type of rigid confusion when encountering bodies in attempts to know the mind. Encountering bodies with minds in this sense can consist of many arrangements, including the psychiatrist encountering the patient's body-mind, the patient encountering their own body-mind, and the psychiatrist encountering their own body-mind. Set in contrast to the rigid confusion are the possibilities that relationality can offer, where confusion and conflict are tolerated and worked through. To assess these problems within psychiatry's education, I return again to Sacks the neurologist, but this time to couple him with Michel

Foucault the historian and Hannah Arendt the philosopher. Odd bedfellows indeed, but together, I argue, they bring an ethical turn in psychiatric education that can be used to engage the grim emotional situation of matricide, the killing of one's mother. I use the term *matricide* symbolically to represent the many difficult situations constituting the arc of psychiatry's history predicated on the absence of women, and a term that paradoxically offers a way through the messy conceptual collisions and polarities associated with the body in education. It is this lethal imaginary space of maternal elimination that ironically sets the stage for the natality of a psychiatrist educator like me, reliant as I am upon my own female body, to question the discourse of a masculine authority. These affecting conditions will serve as the ambit for my interrogation of a life-and-death educational space in my experience of psychiatry.

Masculine Authority and the Psychiatry Phenotype

Where did psychiatric education find its origins? I didn't bother probing this question until the work of this book. I suspect I didn't think I would like what I was certain to find. Perhaps my premature foreclosure on these kinds of curiosities grew out of my childhood in Mennonite Bible Belt southern Manitoba, a place and a time where I was iteratively reminded that my own gendered origins were a sacred act of charity. God apparently did miraculous things in Creation, constructing my very sex from the ribs of a man. I came from Adam. And before Adam, there was only God. Who can argue with that chain of signification? In the Olympics of human life, females are awarded the bronze medal. Shouldn't I just be appreciative that we made it to the winner's podium? Somehow this description has always struck me as disdainful and didn't convey a kind of supernatural, awe-inspiring, celebratory arrival of my female species. The narrative that positioned me as an afterthought made right by a human carcass inevitably inspired within me an emancipatory dreams about a different encounter shaping the body of my genesis.

Moving into a world of academic psychiatry, this nascent desire to become somebody as a woman gave rise to unspoken questions deeply relevant to the problems animating psychiatry's education. How is it that the body can be implicated as the site of a learning encounter in the work of knowing? How is it that we come to think about ways of knowing that will, at times, look like either judgment or authority, or be dependent on relationship for intelligibility? I see medicine acting as its own authority over physicians and patients alike, but also being acted out, in part, by physicians through their judgments. It should come as no surprise then that this form of institutional introjection in which bodies acting as authorities and bodies being acted upon by authoritative acts will do so with an assurance of conflict. I begin here with the question of authority as a problem, particularly as it relates to the practice of psychiatry, which, at first glance, registers as a navigation of concerns of the mind and less so of the body.

My curiosity is therefore directed at the body's emergence as an important site of authority in psychiatry and its import in the practice of the mind.

Foucault is undoubtedly an expert on the problem of authority, particularly in relationship to the history of psychiatry and its education. In his lecture series *Psychiatric Power* (2006), Foucault describes the beginning of psychiatric education, or rather an education of the mind, which started as a fantasy about bodily order. This fantasy was articulated by nineteenth-century French psychiatrist François-Emmanuel Fodéré's description of an ideal asylum, which was interestingly romantic in aesthetic but simultaneously constituted by a set of commitments to the regimented maintenance of psychiatric patients. Foucault writes of this dramatic stage as follows: "What will take place in this setting? Well, of course, order reigns, the law, and power reigns . . . an order reigns in the simple sense of a never ending, permanent regulation of time, activities, and actions; an order which surrounds, penetrates, and works on bodies, applies itself to their surfaces, but which equally imprints itself on the nerves" (2). Foucault suggests that the fabric of the fantasy is "an order, therefore, for which bodies are only surfaces to be penetrated and volumes to be worked on" (2). This type of bodily invasion, not to be mistaken with the intended healing of a surgical incision, is purposed with the installation of calm and order. The paradox at hand is seemingly obvious. Where is repose for the mind when the body is being attacked? This somatic irony is where Foucault begins his overview about the necessary place and penetration of the body in the history of psychiatry and by extension opening to a new vantage point conceptualizing the meaning of the body in psychiatry.

What does the body of a psychiatrist look like? As a point of clarification, I am using the term *psychiatrist* but I am really interested in physicians who are relegated to the work of the mind. This could mean physicians in specialties such as psychiatry, neurology, pediatrics, pain medicine, and so on. In reading Foucault's (2006) account of the earliest descriptions by Fodéré, there is little question about what type of a body belongs to a psychiatrist. Fodéré states,

> Generally speaking, perhaps one of the first conditions of success in our profession is a fine, that is to say, noble and manly physique; it is especially indispensable for impressing the mad. Dark hair, or hair whitened by age, lively eyes, a proud bearing, limbs and chest announcing strength and health, prominent features, and a strong and expressive voice are the forms that generally have a great effect on individuals who think they are superior to everyone else. The mind undoubtedly regulates the body, but this is not apparent to begin with and external forms are needed to lead the multitude. (quoted in Foucault 2006, 4)

The description is striking in its definitive linking of authority to the masculine body, opening to many possible turns and interpretations. At first glance, I have registered that the subject being spoken about is clearly not me. I am immediately caught in a deeply contradictory moment that splits my reality, forcing me to defensively write my way out of a confrontational education that has already erased me. In this moment, Freud's id-ego-superego paradigm helps me to understand, at least in part, what is happening. The anxiety of being erased as a female psychiatrist registers a bit like being buried alive. In this conflict, the ego must negotiate between the id and the superego where the id demands an object of satisfaction — that is, my body as the keeper of my mind. Yet the superego tells me that an idealized self-image must have a mustache and beard (i.e., not me). Education becomes the superego in this scene, enacting a prohibition against the female body.

In registering this historical gendered exclusion, I may generously assume that Fodéré was the product of his time in his proclivity for males to represent psychiatrists, and that time has indeed moved us into another space, more forgiving of myopic stereotypes, open to all genders as well as the creativity implicit in diverse perspectives. But relatively recent publications by Laura Hirshbein (2004), Sophia Frangou (2016), and Resa Lewiss and colleagues (2020) on the history of women in psychiatry or women in academic medicine come to the same conclusion that I am arriving at: in principle, female psychiatrists did not exist until the mid- to late twentieth century. And when women were allowed as physicians, the authors' data point to a psychiatric narrative relegating women to the custodial work of seeing patients and teaching, with limited experience or representation in places of academic advancement, scholarly publications, and leadership that were otherwise normative for males. Education, more broadly speaking, has a penchant for custodial work symptomatic of a troubling cliché. Britzman's *Practice Makes Practice* (2003b) highlights the problem of persisting stereotypes in education that foreclose on the important possibilities inherent in discussions of gender and identity. She states, "In the case of women teachers, who are merely seen to carry their 'natural' abilities into the marketplace, they are apt to be characterized as either martyrs or idiots" (29). Britzman offers a related problematic: "Stereotypes engender a static and hence repressed notion of identity as something already out there, a stability that can be assumed. Here, identity is expressed as a final destination rather than a place of departure" (29). It is oddly exasperating that in 2025 the question of navigating space for women in medicine has not been rendered an artifact of time gone by. As with education, the question of gender identity and the premature stereotypes in medicine have mostly silenced a more critical and inclusive discourse that lies in wait. This absence symbolically aligns with Fodéré's description of bodies that represent psychiatry, resonating as a contemporary belonging, suggesting that gender is indeed a burgeoning and novel idea within the profession.

In returning to where we started this discussion, that is, with Fodéré and an ideal of the male psychiatrist, we are introduced to a figure that will have a permanent arc in psychiatry, first as a hero who will emancipate the psychiatrically unwell from the shackles of the asylum, and then later fulfilling the role as the overseer of the asylum, understood in its contemporary form as the hospital administrator. I will return to the hospital administrator as a masculine dynamic and authority that comes to bear on the question of the gendered problem of authoritative bodies in the work and education of psychiatry later on. In the meantime, permit me a quick memory that is triggered as I write about my female body being relegated to spaces that are both permissible and not permissible, suggesting that Fodéré's thinking is in the DNA of academic psychiatry and my education.

As a psychiatry trainee, I knew that I wanted to pursue the subspecialty of child and adolescent psychiatry. From the start of my postgraduate training, I didn't veer from this goal. Throughout my education, I got to know the clinical and academic leaders within child psychiatry (i.e., all men), from whom I frequently received positive feedback about my ability to engage with patients and was praised for a mind capable of thinking beyond rigid taxonomies characteristic of the knowledge contained in the *Diagnostic and Statistical Manual of Mental Disorders* (DSM). I was venerated both as a clinician and as a potential researcher. In my hesitancy to pursue research at the time of training, I indicated to the academic head that I was hoping to pursue a master's or PhD after I had completed my residency. His response to me was that I would never complete a master's, let alone a PhD after residency. The need to earn money and the demands on female time would not permit this. He did not outright come out and talk about how my children would need me at home — he didn't need to. Further education was simply not in the cards for me, which, by extension, would also silently exclude future academic leadership opportunities. I was later told by the clinical lead that the academic head had taken him aside and shared with him an impression about me, describing me as very, very capable. Capable enough, in fact, that if I worked hard and did not lose sight of what I was in pursuit of, I might even be successful enough to be a program director for postgraduate training in psychiatry. I can assure you that this suggestion was made by him with neither malice nor sarcasm — that was not his way. While I have no misgivings about the importance of medical education and education leadership, it was the unequivocal foreclosure on the idea that I could strive only to be a woman relegated to the custodial work of medicine and its education that was deeply troubling. *My body* would not be *the body* capable of higher education, therefore excluding me from a competition of bodies that may someday oversee or direct his work.

Psychiatric Education and Matricide

Fodéré's text does not leave room for creative imagination about how a woman could fit the bill of what the aggregate body of a psychiatrist is. The described masculine imaginary has been announced as the phenotypic prototype of a psychiatrist, necessarily creating a practice of exclusion for women. Where then can I find myself in the question of the problem of authority as it relates to bodies? At least in the creation story of Adam and Eve, my body registered as a skeletal segment that was, in fact, a somewhat important storyline. According to Fodéré, I was extinct before making it to the psychiatry starting block. The irony of this omission is not lost on me, particularly when there was plenty of room to bring the likes of me and my body as a patient to be worked on by men who dominated psychiatry's profession. A woman's gender mattered significantly when an object was required to engage and cohere a psychiatric practice made specifically for men. As an academic psychiatrist attempting to name the larger phenomenology at play, it is a strange realization to stumble into a historical scenario in which my body acted as its own exclusion criteria only to then realize that there wasn't a question of inclusion criteria in the first place. Something nefarious has surely been attached to my body and, by extension, my mind, to make it a somatic space uninhabitable for me to do what I am currently doing in academic psychiatry.

I am not sure that a climactic, dramatic, and reparative moment has ever occurred declaring Fodéré's rendition of the psychiatrist's body as obsolete, therefore ushering in a new world of psychiatrists in which all bodies and genders are welcomed. To me, it seems as though a different temporality is at play in considering the arc of psychiatric practice where men constituted practice until women were there. It is difficult to really understand the collision course that would see women emerge in this arena. Were women conceded to as an eventual artifact of progress? Alternatively, were they accepted, put up with, or relegated to other identities in their appearance as professional counterparts to the original psychiatrists?

Through these reflections an intensely provocative problem has emerged having to do with my own beginning as a female psychiatrist. Where did I come from? Was I an educational child without an educational mother? How was it that my own psychiatric natality was allowed in a history predicated on exclusion? I am struck by the intellectual veracities of gestation and birth and motherhood captured within these questions, leading to many ways of thinking about the educational question at hand. Was there ever a figure of an educational mother, and if so, what happened to her? The question of my psychiatric natality, my coming into the world of psychiatrists as a female, is paradoxically shaped by a narrative of what was not permitted. The image of a severed umbilical cord emerges for me in this prenatal discourse, pointing to the excision of a symbolic educational mother. I begin to think about my current body as an effect of psychiatry being dependent on a symbolic reckoning of the past and wonder what a "re-birth" might signal. Arendt's "Crisis in Education" (1993) stages a conflict between the newly arrived and those already there, describing the problem of natality as an unwelcome newness in a human world wary of it when she writes,

> Basically, we are always educating for a world that is or is becoming out of joint, for this is the basic human situation, in

> which the world is created by mortal hands to serve mortals for a limited time as home. Because the world is made by mortals, it wears out; and because it continually changes its inhabitants it runs the risk of becoming as mortal as they. To preserve the world against the mortality of its creators and inhabitants, it must be constantly set right anew. (192)

Philosophers are typically thin on the use of emotive or affecting language, but in the above passage, evocative descriptors invite the reader into a shared groaning in which we hear the creaking arthritic joints and we witness the limping, weary from the educational work of anticipating what is to come. It is unusual language for an unusual perspective that catches me off guard. While Arendt is supporting the notion that we as humans come into the world first to begin and not to die, the problem of education turns this on its head. The human condition, according to Arendt, knows only weariness as an effect of education that both anticipates newness and is resistant to renewal. And I wonder here if Arendt is saying that we are born into the world to begin but education metaphorically kills us to protect what is already here. And then perhaps we can get back to the work of beginning. The phenomenon she describes is perhaps why she chose provocative language for the title of her article: a rejection of newness is anathema to the work of education, signifying a crisis indeed. But I want to look past the obvious and take a moment to stay with the following Arendtian quote: "It is in the very nature of the human condition that each new generation grows into an old world, so that to prepare a new generation for a new world can only mean that one wishes to strike from newcomers' hands their own chance at the new" (177). Arendt is clear about what is at stake. In using the term *strike* a danger is exerted and a kind of potential lethality introduced. Another way of animating the text is to ventriloquize what I think I am hearing, which is "We will snuff out your newness to prepare you for a world that only has hostility for anything other than what already is." I am reminded of a conversation that I had with a colleague whom I was talking to about the burden of being junior faculty and how its reality was palpable for me in different parts of the university experience. She shared with me, in hushed tones, a statement made to her by a senior male faculty member that she had never forgotten. "We eat our young in this department," he had said to her. This notion of academic cannibalism reverberates in my thinking about gendered bodies being determined structures of historicity in the discourse of psychiatric education. Applying Arendt's thinking, the mother of all women who would arrive on the scene of psychiatry as a psychiatrist has been fatally eliminated to protect what was already there. Her elimination can be thought of as a form of educational matricide.

Alice Pitt (2006) suggests that the idea of matricide can be understood, in part, as cultural commentary. She tackles the importance of the stark and unsettling concept of matricide in her essay "Mother Love's Education" where the murder of one's mother as a symbolic or mythical act of the mind can be explored through different orientations. Similar to Pitt, I too offer observations of matricide understood primarily as a cultural object under threat, but also return to the idea of relationality to ask, What can the nature of the relationship with the maternal, even when she is absent, show me about my body and my encounter with an education of exclusion?

My first reactions to the idea of matricide can best be described as a petulant state of childlike regression in registering rejection and exclusion of myself. The history of losses I have stumbled into — the realization that my body never belonged, specifically as a consequence of matricide — translates into a psychical scene where I find myself shrieking the accusation at a host of nameless, faceless male psychiatrists, "You killed me!" But this peevish emotional eruption finds its way into a more productive encounter with matricide when Pitt (2006) suggests that matricide is less about settling the score as a point of feminist debate and more about the pressing question of why and what remains in the aftermath of this symbolic event. Speaking in currencies of symbolism, particularly the importance of symbolism in the case of matricide, Pitt tells us: "Symbolization, a process that traverses cycle and external reality as well as thought and fantasy, takes the act of naming the world to a deeper level where one is able to reflect upon one's representations. To put it another way, we use language to represent to ourselves and to others, objects, concepts, and affects" (88).

Pitt's (2003) understanding of the importance of symbolism in its portrayal of matricide as an educational idea is unexpectedly generative despite the associated lethality. In offering a way to "name the world to a deeper level," she writes past Arendt's conundrum and beautifully builds another set of handrails for me to hang on to as I navigate further into the educational depths of Fodéré's bodily exclusion of female psychiatrists. While Pitt's focus is on what it means to bring the mother into different forms of representation, her focus on matricide as a cultural artifact is helpful in thinking about Fodéré's description. Pitt speaks to an exclusion of women from culture and history where "matricide is represented as a trauma of history that inaugurates women's social status as inferior and subject to laws and knowledge made for and by men" (89). In the earliest accounts of psychiatry, Pitt's language could not ring truer. She goes on to state, "The problem of representation of the mother is her absence from representation, and matricide is a means by which her absence is assured" (89).

Pitt (2003) later uses the word *erasure* (92) as a fitting metaphor describing the grand matricide that cheated women of a beginning. I now apply this term to my thinking about a sense of natality for female psychiatrists. The discourse of masculine normalization relying on a historical erasure of females has also acted to strengthen the effects of the masculine fantasy that constituted the erasure. This kind of invisibility relegates me to a part of psychiatry that continues to be without recognizable morphology. Something about the historical account provided by Foucault (2006) threatens me, and my reaction tells me that there is more at stake than the practice of reading a historical text. But a crisis is perhaps the educational point that is trying to make its way to me, reminiscent of Arendt's essay title, as I stumble through what is mostly felt, almost inaccessible to language in making meaning. There is no existential crisis at hand. I clearly exist as a female psychiatrist in the here and now, but somehow I have not yet made it to the starting line. My entrance to or beginning at the scene is belated and continues to be belated in a practice of academic exclusions. But the idea of beginning as a consequence of ending is precisely what I think Arendt is getting at when it comes to education. It is somehow fitting that the idea of matricide is responded to with the language of natality — a kind of antiphonal call from the grave of the mother to her innate, generative ability. Educational theorist Natasha Levinson (1997) builds on Arendt's idea of natality: "The world does not simply precede us but effectively constitutes us as particular kinds of people. The resulting social identities position us in relation to one another, to the past and to the future in particular ways, putting us in a difficult position of being simultaneously heirs to a specific history and new to it. As a result, we experience ourselves as "belated" even though we are newcomers" (437). Those who are new are already old, and those who receive newcomers already symbolically hate them and wish for their end. Similarly, the newcomers must hate those that get in their way. This problem registers as a weight that the medical profession carries from having grown out of a practice of exclusion. Here, an opening occurs to understand an antagonistically inherited non-space signified by a body that is not mine but also finds a way around the messiness of trying to get into a game where I am not invited to play.

If I return to Arendt, reading with another orientation, I believe she hints at an alternative to the hostility directed at another's newness, which consists of an intersubjective orientation more tempered in its approach to newness and boils down to relationship. Arendt (1993) suggests that the task of education is "always to cherish and protect something — the child against the world, the world against the child, the new against the old, the old against the new" (192). In this quote, I believe that Arendt is commenting on a relational tension that contains the constant risk of destruction, but also implies that something generative can simultaneously come from understanding this tension. If I turn to my psychiatrist voice, I do not want my newcomer status as a woman to destroy the education of psychiatry and its past because I continue to practice within the arena, which has a history including those before me. But I also need to find a new version of myself that can remain in the balance of new and old. Levinson suggests that one can engage acts of "self-creation in relation to the world that preceded us and to which we respond" (439). In other words, I can't change the past by changing a past where I didn't exist, but I still have the chance to exist.

Before I feel reassured, there is another problem at hand that has to do with knowledge and its knower in this discussion of psychiatry, education, natality, and matricide. Although both knowledge and the knower in psychiatry have historically been relegated to the bodies of males, my arrival as a woman psychiatrist shines a spotlight on another psychiatric lacuna as a symptom of matricide. The idea of matricide says that even if murdered, the symbolic mother is affected in this equation of knowing and knower. A feminine orientation would suggest that knowledge is always relational in its situation with the knower. However, in severing the relation between knowledge and the knower as a gendered effect of matricide, we are left with another educational tension having to do with natality, where natality itself is compromised. It is a metaphorical interpretation where the birth of the baby has been aborted or where conditions give way to habitual stillbirth, as they can never know their own natality. We arrive to end again, as per Arendt's position in "The Crisis in Education" (1993), in an attempt to know. Newness will not be tolerated, even if it signals an attempt to bind together the thought to the thinker who inhabits a body, ironically essential in its role as placeholder for knowledge in psychiatry.

To summarize where I think I land in this dizzying discourse, always seemingly at the edges of danger, I can or must creatively constitute a new kind of relational space for and with myself as a woman psychiatrist educator. I also think Levinson is suggesting education as a kind of relational engagement to address the body barrier. This, to me, means a commitment to recognizing and exploring our deep intra- and intersubjectivities that would lead us beyond contemporary conversations predicated on and paralyzed by gender. It is here where I can encounter myself anew, no longer fearing retaliation, but as an independent, autonomous being who is free to think and know, and create relationships, even with what has been destroyed. In doing so, a new economy of educational relationship is being created that will also figure into a number of Sacks's accounts of his own body in education and its associations with the concept of matricide.

Brains versus Brawn versus Heart

At this point in time, I want to return to where I began. One of the three main problems mentioned at the start of this chapter had to do with authority and judgment in relation to understanding the place of the body in education. I want to pause and engage the problem of judgment as a form of authority, and then look at authority as an act of judgment. I am using these terms interchangeably, although it seems to me that they are quite different in their opening of the problem of the body in psychiatry and in their provocations as related to education in psychiatry. I also want to return to Foucault's (2006) observations about the role of authority relating to the gendered body as a way of bringing us to a different set of gendered ideas enacted within Sacks's experience of taking care of his own body as well as using it in the service of others.

Implied in Fodéré's description of masculine physician authority and its purpose is a relationship of power harkening back to a more primitive time where might was right and human survival depended on it. Foucault (2006) made note of this kind of militarization of language through images of powerful conflicts between the psychiatrist and the patient. However, in Foucault's scenes of the beginning of psychiatry, or what he will call "proto-psychiatry" (8), it is not only the body of patient, however big or small, masculine or feminine, that registered as a threat. Rather, a mind presumed to be unwell should be feared, particularly if the owner's mind did not concede to the Goliath of supervision that surrounded it. But in Foucault's account of scenes of supervision within the asylum, it is the supervisor's body whose physique paradoxically mattered in corralling the psychiatric patient's wandering mind. This physique again constitutes both inclusion and exclusion criteria for physician bodies that matter. The description of masculinity offered by Fodéré introduces a practice of masculinity that has taken up the matter of brains versus brawn versus heart and has settled its own score. The body of the physician is not intended for therapeutics directed at thought and feeling. Rather, the physician's power is called upon as a necessary act of force to do battle with the dangerous minds of patients whose sickness will relegate them to the status of an unwieldy subordinate. In this scenario, the patient has been set up to talk back to the doctor's power with an unwelcome voice. However, it is the patient's body that will be managed in a silencing act. A psychiatrist's body in this historical account is subjected to and becomes the subject of a physical conflict with the unwell mind, presenting itself as a warning sign. This morphological signal is also educational in nature. What does the body need to do in the bodily work and relationality of being a doctor of the mind? Presumably, get bigger.

Sacks (2016) too was aware of this somatic signal to increase his size, either consciously or unconsciously. In his memoir, Sacks goes to great lengths to tell us about his preoccupation with weight lifting and how it oriented him toward his own mind. Olympic-level weights became a point of welcome distraction for him, and his body responded in kind to a heroic call in the need to get larger. He writes with admiration about an Olympic weight lifter with whom he was training. Sacks says, "He had enormous thighs and was a world-class squatter. I admired his squatting ability, and I too wanted to develop such thighs" (99). It will become clear to Sacks later on that there is a link in his mind between succeeding physically and succeeding as an academic physician. Sacks writes about the reasons behind his frenzied, maniacal efforts in weight lifting almost as a footnoted afterthought. In what reads as a guilty admission, Sacks states, "I sometimes wonder why I pushed myself so relentlessly in weightlifting. My motive, I think, was not an uncommon one; I was not the ninety-eight-pound weakling of bodybuilding advertisements, but I was timid, diffident, insecure, submissive. I became strong — very strong — with all my weightlifting but found that this did nothing for my character, which remained exactly the same" (122). Prior to this, he acknowledges that to set a record in powerlifting, which he did, was the equivalent "to publishing a scientific paper or a book in academia" (101). Something prized is associated with a Herculean strength that Sacks was alive to. His reflections point to a kind of internal chastising where I could imagine him saying to himself, "Sacks, man up and brace yourself." In other words, the real work of a physician at the start of psychiatry is to literally *man up*. An educational curriculum in psychiatry is therefore made of testosterone and dumbbells.

But for Sacks, this strategy failed. Sort of. Sacks laments his degenerating body while in hospital recovering from extensive weight-lifting injuries. He is visited by a powerlifting hero and friend who hobbles into Sacks's hospital room. Sacks (2016) says, "We looked at each other, our bodies half-destroyed by lifting" (122). And yet prior to this depiction, Sacks talks about using his body and his strength in acts of healing, a description that would otherwise be assumed in Fodéré's account, although falls short as a therapeutic function in the zeitgeist of psychiatric historicity.

In between his internship and residency at UCLA, at the height of his weight-lifting efforts, Sacks goes back to England and visits his parents, whom he had not seen for two years. He writes of the delicate precariousness of carrying his mother up and down the steep, rickety stairs in their England home after she fractures her hip: "Our winding staircase, with worn carpet and sometimes loose stair rods, was not safe for someone on crutches, so I carried her up and down as she needed — she had been against my heavy lifting, but now she was glad of my strength" (101–102). The image of his behemoth of a body in the reverse role of mother converges on another idea of how the physician's body might relate within medicine. It is this moment that is cause for pause. As I return to the idea of authority and matricide, I use Sacks's account to act as a hinge for me to think further. He is obviously using the strength and size of his body, similar to the descriptions by Fodéré. But Sacks's use of his body is much more than his brute physicality. The aesthetic in his description points to a beautiful and tender emotional logic at play, taking us out of his body and into his mind, while not leaving his heart behind. Sacks's use of his body here can be read as a physical enactment of natality, affectively engaged such that there is a newness in the letting go or a moving beyond the confines of a masculine male whose body is used only as an act of strength to enforce authoritative judgments. At the same time, Sacks somatically embodies natality through his ability to hold the negative capability represented in the frailty that is his mother. He is using his body as a placeholder for uncertainty and the pain associated with clutching at what cannot be grasped, and in doing so, Sacks brings us to the idea of embodied uncertainty as a generative place of possibility. The work of carrying simultaneously acts as a conceptual hinge for us in thinking about the embodied intersectionality of natality and negative capability, particularly in relationship to matricide as an authority, but also alerting us to the kind of personal dance that Sacks is showing us.

There are two orientations that are notable for me; first, matricide as it applies to Sacks's mother, and second, matricide as an experience for Sacks. On the one hand, there is a clear vulnerability for Sacks's mother, whose body is being portrayed as frail and dangerously lifeless in this text. Only Sacks's body is animated, and whether he is carrying her to life or to death as he traverses the rickety steps is unknown to him at the time. His writing here feels like a harbinger of her death, as if he is carrying the one who gave him life symbolically to this place beyond life. On the other hand, perhaps a more generative perspective in this scene is thinking about matricide as an orientation to understand Sacks's body. Here he discovers the use of his large, muscular body as not only male but also as not male. It is interesting to read how his description of himself in physical relationship with his mother brings him to a body, or a feminine embodiment, that is more of a home for him. He is cradling his mother in this tender scene, like a mother would cradle a child, in an act of giving life. The scene can be thought of as Sacks carrying her to give her life, bringing to the fore the notion that what the mother's body is for is anathema to what is going on in the hospital. In other words, physicality is used as a container for caring as opposed to corralling. We see this in the following additional examples in which Sacks uses his strength as another kind of body, quite literally, within his role as physician. One scenario is a patient's neurological crisis due to intracerebral pressure, where the patient's brain stem is pushed into the opening at the base of the skull, an opening never intended to be a conduit for the passage of backward flow of brain matter into the spinal column. Sacks (2016) says, "With the speed of reflex I grabbed our patient and held him upside down; his cerebellar tonsils and brain stem went back into the skull, and I felt I had snatched him from the very jaws of death" (121). His physical strength also appears in another scenario in which he is working with a young woman on a hospital ward who was without sight and paralyzed. She was in a palliative state, waiting to die. She finds out that Sacks has a motorbike and tells him that her dying wish is to go on a ride with him. Sacks writes, "I came to the hospital one Sunday with three weightlifting buddies, and we managed to abduct the patient and lash her securely to me on the back of the bike. I set out slowly and gave her the ride . . . she desired. There was outrage when I got back, and I thought I would be fired on the spot. But my colleagues — and the patient — spoke up for me, and I was strongly cautioned but not dismissed" (122). Here, the body acting as an authority again suggests a symbolic feminine relationality that is both maternal and mythical in her strength to carry not only herself but others. The work of carrying and being carried signals a different positioning of bodies bringing to the fore the image of the mother and child holding tight, one to another. It is interesting to note the dynamic movement in each of these scenarios shared by Sacks, movement that is both emancipating and medicinal. In the act of carrying, one gets the sense that he is cradling the potential that is life itself — an homage to natality that is also simultaneously introduced through the uncertainty embodied within negative capability. These images are in stark contrast to the one-dimensional, static images offered by Fodéré.

I too have used my female body as a psychiatrist, perhaps not in dramatic ways described by Sacks, but in the maternal ways rendered in Sacks's images. I was recently on call and was phoned by the nurse in charge about a homeless adolescent who was wanting to leave the emergency department. The patient had been to the hospital many times before, and it had repeatedly been a traumatizing experience for her. She wanted to leave and at the same time had nowhere to go. It was close to midnight when I got the call from the nurse, keen to demonstrate his knowledge about the mental health act. He wanted me to know that the patient stated an intention to leave and that he had an ethical obligation to tell her what her various options were, including going to a shelter, being discharged to the street, calling family members who had dropped her off at the emergency department stating that she was not welcome in their home, or calling in the on-call doctor to place her on a form insisting on a short hospital stay because of safety concerns. All of the options presented to me did not sound like options at all.

I found myself frustrated with the ineptitude or willful obstruction on the part of the nurse in managing a common problem in this setting that had a relatively common solution. Of course the teen wanted to leave the hospital. This was to be expected. Teens need to be listened to and engaged to understand the resistance. A conversation is what it boiled down to. I got out of my pajamas and dressed myself with an angry invigoration, wanting to believe that this was a human situation with a humane solution as opposed to a mental health crisis requiring psychiatric legislation. When I arrived at the hospital it was well past 1 a.m. I asked the patient for her permission to enter her room. She told me that she wanted to leave but sounded deflated and lackluster in her sense of urgency. I relayed an appreciation of her desire to be elsewhere and asked her what the hospital surroundings felt like for her. She told me of being in the hospital at previous times, being bored, being locked in her room, being afraid that she would never see her pet lizard, who was the only living being that gave her comfort at bedtime. I clued in. Tell me about your lizard. How does your lizard help you at bedtime? What does it feel like to have your lizard with you at bedtime? He tucks me in, she said. He cuddles in beside my head. He tells me I am okay.

Although I find the thought of a reptile beside my own head entirely repulsive, the youth had brilliantly conveyed to me what she needed, and I thanked her for having a lizard who was clever enough to instruct the doctor in finding good enough options for her. I offered to get her some warm blankets, a snack, a bedside light, and possibly an object that reminded her of her lizard. She agreed and told me that she was willing to stay for the night, and then added a half-hearted proviso that her conditions for staying were contingent on going home the next day. We both did not need to state the obvious; home was a fantasy. When I came back with my doctor's bag full of everyday items, she looked at me with fearful eyes, dull yet with a penetrating longing that I couldn't quite explain. I returned to talking about her lizard and she shyly asked if she could be tucked in, like her lizard would do for her. I agreed and almost instantly was deeply uncomfortable in that moment, realizing that I had potentially agreed to a response beyond an acceptable boundary. I was not quite sure how she would want to be tucked in. What if the need was too great? How would I be asked to use my body? She knew better than I did and told me it was only her feet that needed the blankets tucked around them. This is what her lizard would do.

This act of bedtime ritual therapeutics never anticipated as a relational point of adolescent clinical care, and never spoken about in medical training, I do with my body. I am not like Sacks in that there are no acts of neurological greatness, no heroic granting of last wishes; rather, a simple attending to what a lizard would have done. But I am like Sacks using my body for connection and healing. In this scene, I wonder if the authority attached to my physician status moved closer to the effects of natality where my clinical expertise and judgment were informed by the idea of a caring lizard. In the moments that followed, recognizing that the actions of a lizard described by the patient were really acts of imagination about the need for her care led me to stop and think. This pause can be thought of as a kind of gestational period, deeply informed precisely by the intersubjectivity that was taking place between the patient, her fantasies about what she needed, and me. The net result proved to be educationally and clinically generative. This relational place of discovery and thought departure would be a trope that I would return to as I moved through other educational experiences.

Four

Hospital People

On the heels of discovering an educational mother, paradoxically through a discourse on matricide, educational space now offers the possibility of deep relationality. But my ability to rely on relationship throughout my medical training and practice will be tested by many places and people that constitute the work of medicine. We now arrive at the hospital and move through the entrance doors, where the smells of sickness and the dizzying institutional space of bedpans, seclusion rooms, and call bells seemingly dispossesses the conditions of educational work where affecting newness is to begin. As an academic psychiatrist, education would often paradoxically be experienced like vestiges of the sterile surroundings, eventually prompting me to instruct student doctors to abandon the diagnostic interview and work toward a shared, authentic exploration of psychical suffering. However, this invitation has repeatedly been viewed as too risky in its uncomfortable departure from practices predicated on symptomatic inevitability and would be tolerated by the students only as an isolated event at trying to practice psychiatry in a nonconventional way. Efforts to work toward a practice exodus where I would leave questions of diagnostics behind and work toward an understanding of suffering have repeatedly felt as though an educational undertow was present, making the hospital almost anaphylactic to its own directive for caring. In this observation, the function of the hospital becomes fused or infused with the image of a physician offered by François-Emmanuel Fodéré: mechanistic in form and a static presence. Fodéré's physician can be seen as a symbolic placeholder that remains present in the activities of the hospital until something else happens in a series of foregone conclusions. In Fodéré's hospital, patients are to be affected upon and led away from themselves, suggesting a type of relational deficiency that leaves an industrial taste in our mouths.

In contrast to images suggested by Fodéré, Oliver Sacks's (2016) writing resonates with my own search for meaning in clinical work and highlights a kind of deep relationality that he encounters with patients as well as discovering an embedded reciprocity with them. He begins these descriptions by writing, "As soon as I started clinical work in October 1966, I felt better. I found my patients fascinating, and I cared for them. I started to taste my own clinical and therapeutic powers and, above all, the sense of autonomy and responsibility which I had been denied when I was still a resident in training" (146). It would seem logical to think that a successful physician such as Sacks would have been well regarded by the hospital administrators, as it only stands to reason that physician performance has the potential to show the administrator in a positive light. For Sacks, his clinical success was a liability. Sacks's acts of caring and engagement would repeatedly draw ire from the hospital administrators to whom he reported. The scene in which Sacks responds to a patient's dying wish for a motorcycle ride and almost loses his job becomes a type of imprinted map unconsciously steering him away from the constraints imposed by administrative tensions, which can be translated into contemporary realities in medicine consisting of best practices, quality control, and accountability measures. There is a clear sense of duality that emerges for Sacks throughout his memoir as it relates to the medical arena: there are hospital people, many of whom are also physicians, and then there is everyone else. In highlighting this binary, I am trying to lay bare the challenge at hand. Specifically, what is it about the historical positioning of bodies within the hospital (i.e., asylum) that renders an intelligibility in contemporary education for my own body as a female physician interested in working with questions of the mind?

I keep Sacks close to me as I delve into this question of meaning. I read his story as my own to open the idea of how past renderings of the psychiatrist as a function of the asylum may not be as rarified as one might think. Sacks provides many examples about his encounters with hospital administration that position him in particular ways, opening to new dynamics that speak to an oblique educational valence shaping Sacks's practice. In his first outpatient clinical experience as a consulting neurologist for a migraine clinic, he describes a meaningful clinical engagement with patients that captures both his intellect and his imagination. He is singled out by the clinical head of the migraine clinic, who likely saw Sacks's potential and wanted to play a mentoring role for him. But the mentee outsmarted the mentor, literally and symbolically, when Sacks wrote a book on migraines that was subsequently plagiarized by his boss. Sacks was threatened to stay away from any more academic writing pursuits and was eventually fired for his success. For Sacks, his caring was an academic pursuit but over time simultaneously became an act of profound resistance to the administrative structure around him, which ironically had academic ties. If this experience resulted in a justified mistrust and deep paranoia about those who were supposed to see him succeed, Sacks does not outright comment. However, this profound betrayal likely acted as a type of educational protype suggesting that hypervigilance was required for Sacks's safety and survival. He continues to set up scenes he will encounter with various hospital people in which we find him at odds with an infrastructure that is intended to promote his caring.

Awakenings

In late 1960s, Sacks began independent clinical practice at Beth Abraham, a five-hundred-bed chronic care facility where he rehearses the role of a patient, living among those he was responsible for. It is important to be cognizant of the fact that this hospital would most likely have looked like an asylum prior to deinstitutionalization, which occurred in the early 1970s. Sacks was willing to make an asylum, a place occupied by the outcast and left behind, his home. It was at this time that he famously became interested in a group of individuals with postencephalopathic symptoms that rendered them chronically locked into frozen, parkinsonian states. Sacks attended to the patients with a kind of careful consideration and intellectual granularity that was, and is, uncommon in chronic care settings, where long-standing clinical problems are frequently managed with the passing of time. These patients would be the inspiration for Sacks's investigative research, leading to the dramatic events of recovery and a type of awakening captured in his book *Awakenings* (1990). In this setting he curates his own medical exclusion, finds a home where he negotiates living accommodations on the hospital grounds, and welcomes the nurses, therapists, custodians, and patients, many of whom were his friends. I am sure that most if not all the staff at Beth Abraham liked the idea of having access to the physician scientist among them. His choice to live alongside their work would have signaled a different kind of physician investment and would have marked a practice of nonconformity. It must have been strange, and almost dangerous for Sacks, on some level, to arrive at the place where he could deeply engage with patients, having been castigated for his caring in the past. However, it may have been the only place where he felt as though he was protected from hospital administrators, those that had both criticized and threatened his practice. While Sacks camouflaged himself in patient care on patient grounds, he may have relied on a prediction that hospital administrators would leave him alone, as they had historically done with patients, instead relying on supervision at a distance.

Sacks (2016) had conflicted relationships with many hospital administrators, primarily over his clinical engagement with patients, although his philosophy about education would prime us to understand the impending skirmishes that would iteratively occur with hospital people. As he describes it,

> At one point, the neurology department asked me to test and grade my students. I submitted the requisite form, giving all of them A's. My chairman was indignant. "How can they all be A's?" he asked. "Is this some kind of joke?" I said, no, it wasn't a joke, but the more I got to know each student, the more he seemed to me distinctive. My A was not some attempt to affirm a spurious equality but rather an acknowledgement of the uniqueness of each student. I felt that a student could not be reduced to a number or a test, any more than a patient could. (181)

Sacks's retort to his administrator would have us know that the disagreements he experienced went well beyond differences of clinical opinion, offering an expanded argument inciting a compromised fantasy of physician bodies that most were likely not prepared to acknowledge. Recall Fodéré's attributes of a physician: a big scary body, described with almost militaristic qualities in his ability to block the exit door when patients might be unruly and seeking escape. Sacks's positioning of his body in very maternal ways defied this call to arms. He provides numerous examples of encounters with hospital people in which a litany of his supposed aggressions are directed at him. On one occasion during a strike at Beth Abraham when patients were left without routine care, Sacks would call on his medical students and organize a round-the-clock response for immobilized patients who required turning, toileting, or physiotherapy. He willingly moved past the picket line to act as nurse, therapist, custodian, and physician. At the end of the ten-day strike, he found his car window smashed, with a note stating both that he is loved and that he is a strikebreaker.

During his time at Beth Abraham, Sacks is also chastised for his academic publications. His research findings were met with castigation and hostility by physicians affronted at the suggestion of experimental success solely observed by Sacks but not otherwise witnessed by experts in the field. Sacks (2016) writes, "I had cast doubt on predictability itself" (178) as one explanation for the academic aggression and animosity chronically aimed at him. After three years of intense service at Beth Abraham, Sacks returned from a holiday to England to find that an administrator had evicted him from his hospital grounds apartment because the administrator's mother was unwell and required housing. When attempting to defend the arrangement made with him to remain in the apartment, particularly to maintain close contact with his patients, Sacks writes, "My answer irked the director, who said that because I was questioning his authority, I could leave the apartment *and* the hospital" (191–192). In the wake of his dismissal from Beth Abraham, he was offered a job at Bronx State Hospital on Ward 23, caring for adolescents with autism, schizophrenia, and intellectual delays. When he was given permission to take out a young man named Steve who was described as nonverbal, autistic, and chronically institutionalized, Sacks returned with reports that the outing had been successful despite staff predictions of disastrous outcomes. Sacks described staff as resentful and writes that staff "seemed furious at our description of Steve's good behavior and obvious happiness in the garden and his uttering his first word. We were greeted with black looks" (212). Sacks is then accused of undermining a successful behavioral modification program by offering opportunities for play as a distraction from the conditioned framework that would otherwise guide therapeutics. Sacks notes, "I replied, defending the importance of play and criticizing the reward-punishment model. I said I thought this constituted a monstrous abuse of the patients in the name of science and sometimes smacked of sadism" (212–213). On the heels of this encounter, Sacks is accused of sexually abusing young patients. This profoundly destructive encounter with his colleagues demanded an affecting price for Sacks that most cannot appreciate. Sacks's poignant descriptions of being antagonistically oriented — ironically not toward the illnesses he was taught to treat — but rather with people who represent places of healing, I turn to my own personal interpretations of what it is like to be in relationship with representations of authority.

The Suffering Physician

I too had dark moments within the confines of the hospital and with hospital people. Particular memories are so painful that they are best tucked away, at least for now. Some experiences had to do with my clinical errors being publicly discovered and finding no gentle place to heed them, despite the rhetoric of quality improvement, which typically suggests that opportunities for understanding and improvement are promoted in the wake of a hospital error, as opposed to blaming the individual. Others had to do with challenging calcified pedagogies or advocating for medical learners who, in my mind, were at the behest of a big, indifferent machine relying on their assumed service and simultaneously paying little attention to the meaning of an education of service. Still others had to do with speaking up for patients in a psychiatric system that would commonly aggress against them. I use the term *hospital people* not to speak of particular or specific people but rather representatives of the effects of a failed system that cannot reliably be counted on, or is often resolutely resistant to the suggestion of transformative correction. The examples described above are far more normative than they are outliers in my experience. It tires me to think about narrating the all-too-common conflicts that primarily center around the task of trying to bridge the deeply human with hospital sterility that can be felt similarly as residue of the asylum. At first glance, these partners, that is, the human and the asylum, are not particularly well suited for each other. Sacks seems to have the stomach for it, perhaps because he course-corrected early on and did not orient his clinical compass to an institutional or historical body. He had patients and writing as a distracting aesthetic, a life-preserving reprieve. It is the hospital people moments that instantly drain any reserve of creativity or life for me, and so I have learned that they are best avoided, as Sacks also likely learned.

I am quite sure the hospital people did not know what to make of Sacks, and in fairness, perhaps Sacks was also confused about what was really happening in his altercations with them. What has become clearer to me in studying these encounters described by Sacks is the utility of drawing upon a psychoanalytic interpretation of how the hospital and its people function. Otherwise said, the hospital (and its representatives) is often a defense against the suffering that is apparent, suffering that ranges in expression and articulation. It can act as a giant place for denial and does so with an admirable efficiency such that repudiation is kept far at bay. Coming back to the notion of matricide, we can also see that the efficiency of the hospital as a mechanism of male supervision and authority that also offers an effective defense against thinking about women. It enacts the very historical conditions that often create a cultural space of forgetfulness about the symbolic mother.

In turning again to the idea of hospital culture, the physician, conceptualized as a casualty of this paragon, has only recently begun to be recognized, albeit through the lens or discourse of physician burnout, stress, and inducements for individual resilience. I am talking about something related to burnout but different, something more penetrating and riskier in its affecting depths of self-other relationality prone to residing in the wild places of the unconscious or the concealed. I am reminded of a recent physician suicide widely reported in the context of COVID-19. Dr. Lorna Breen was the head of an emergency department in New York during the recent pandemic. She was the posterchild for perennial success and achievement in medicine. She was also heralded as a physician who was compassionate and deeply committed to her patients. The predictability and control that had made her leadership so successful were all but obliterated in the pandemic. After a brief hospitalization for depression, she killed herself. The *New York Times* (Knoll, Rothfeld, and Watkins 2020) wrote, "If Dr. Breen is lionized along with the legions of other health care workers who gave so much — maybe too much — of themselves, then her shattered family also wants her to be saluted for exposing something more difficult to acknowledge: the culture within the medical community that makes suffering easy to overlook or hide; the trauma that doctors comfortably diagnose, but are reluctant to personally reveal, for fear of ruining their careers" (para. 92).

The devastation in this testimony forms the emotional rubble of a prohibition to speak past the message that physicians are not to speak about themselves. I hear the advice of my mentor in my mind. She often says to me, "Write in first-person narrative. Stay close to the texts you encounter when you write back." Yet my instinct is to distance myself from my own mind, my own body, my own education, and to write around these experiences with the option to meander into an obscurity where my own subjectivity has the option of getting lost and never returning. This wasn't always the case for me. Medicine cemented a kind of self-sterilization, where intimate subjectivity in writing would not be permitted and would also be intuitively difficult to negotiate in the discourse of myself in clinical encounters, in the work of the hospital, or even in medical education. It is clear that something about writing in first person is an irritation, or even ominous for me, although it has been difficult to diagnose. Or perhaps this is less of a diagnostic dilemma and more denial. What is clear is that I don't want to see my own suffering as a physician. I don't want the mirror of Dr. Breen's story held up in front of me to reflect a disease chronicity with an insidious lethality that could be my own, even if it is only relegated to the metaphorical. Why my resistance to the mirror? Ironically, as a psychiatrist who is trained in the working and healing of the mind, I have a fragile uncertainty about my own mind being broken or lost. I don't have the knowledge or the skills to do advanced resuscitation on my psyche if it shatters. This dilemma registers as the tragic impossibility of Humpty Dumpty: once he falls apart, the putting back together again is a fantasy. And this fantasy brings us back to the beginning of Michel Foucault's (2006) lectures about psychiatry, where we find the resisting conflicts in the form of bodies denied and also relied upon. Perhaps the question of the psychiatrist's body and its relationship to the body of the patient is the true stronghold of psychiatry, palpable in the beginning, distracting us from our own minds and from the work of minding our patients' psychical realities. Here the fantasy forecloses on the capacity to imagine, or more specifically engage an imagination of an embodied mind having the fortitude to go beyond its somatic confines. Instead, the fantasy leads us in a direction having to do with militant beliefs about controlling bodies through patient supervision. And this very space is where the authority of the body constitutes a culture equally susceptible to its own illness.

Iatrogenics and Scenes of Supervision

Foucault's (2006) lectures on psychiatric power help me understand the Byzantine world of contemporary psychiatric practice and the ways its practice denies its order. He architecturally locates the space of the psychiatric ward, its people, and its hospital function with compelling descriptions. I recall being a new graduate when my clinical boss approached me. He had plans to open the biggest child and adolescent inpatient ward in the country in our very own academic hospital. At the time I was really quite naive about the politics at play and the subsequent resources involved with the development and delivery of hospital services. My preoccupation then had to do with a clinical understanding informed by training, which interestingly had not included a tertiary level, inpatient experience in child and adolescent psychiatry. I suppose I thought that the training experience I had undergone intentionally omitted inpatient services as a philosophical and moral imperative. Why create a place, such as a locked hospital unit, where young people could enter and be adversely affected by the act of entering? Any door opening to this psychiatric service constituted an agenda about child and youth mental health counter to what was empirically preferred — at least, so I thought. I couldn't have been more wrong. In his rationale for opening a locked unit, clichéd catchphrases such as *early intervention, antistigmatization, patient-centered care, avoiding institutionalization,* and *community-based engagements* were used. I realized that clinical terms he used translated into a type of rhetoric that I now understood was at play. I recall saying to my boss, alive with indignation, "How can we do this? How can we open a psychiatric ward for children and youth? This is iatrogenics at work!" As I understand the term, *iatrogenics* refers to an illness that is acquired within the hospital through common hospital processes, such as providing medical treatment. A frequently cited example is a hospital-acquired infection. But there are other ways in which undergoing hospital care makes people unwell, such as the simple act of admitting a person to a hospital. A sick role is naturally assigned to the person who is now referred to as a patient, and by assigning the natural sick role, the hospital constitutes its power to suggest or cause or illness when illness may not have existed prior to the hospital entrance. I had learned the word *iatrogenics* in training and found its relevance to be more widespread than I could have imagined.

If we build it, they will come, and if they're not sick when they arrive, they will be sick when they leave. And what do we know about the kind of cure needed for a sickness that we, as hospital people, are responsible for?

I was dumbstruck with the undoing at hand. I was perhaps more stunned to find this segment written by Foucault (2006) twenty years earlier yet clearly describing my observations: "Psychiatry says, more of less: 'let your mad little children come to me,' or, 'you're never too young to be mad,' or, 'don't wait for the age of majority or adulthood to be mad.' And all of this is translated into the institutions of supervision, detection, training, and child therapy that you see developing at the end of the nineteenth century" (125). The ward did get built and was subsequently opened with fanfare and photo opportunities for politicians and hospital administrators alike. I needed a job, and this was the only one being offered to me at the time. I became one of the inaugural child and adolescent psychiatrists working on the largest inpatient child and adolescent psychiatry ward in Canada.

The opening and subsequent occupying of space was fascinating, mostly because the common discourse by most was discursively anchored to questions of surveillance. Where would the "care desk" be positioned to have optimal vision? Where would the cameras be? How could we use the space to ensure that children and youth were frequently monitored and rarely out of sight? What kind of observation levels would allow for close proximity at all times? And while I am not critical of the need for observation, there was a kind of perseveration about it as a clinical idea that has philosophical and educational implications.

One of the more recent forms of supervision I have noticed on the ward is a kind of absence. That is, isolation. It is a technique used when youth who are observed to have secondary gain from the hospital social milieu, presumably lose sight of their own therapeutic work. Otherwise said, they are having too good of a time and are thought to demonstrate too little improvement as a result of too many communal distractions on the ward. These youth are therapeutically assigned to *independent work*, which requires them to complete paper-and-pencil tasks in their rooms. But these youth also frequently struggle with deliberate self-harm in the form of cutting themselves and experience intense chronic suicidal ideation, often in response to the disorienting emotional distress associated with rejection or perceived abandonment or trauma. Although one would be hard-pressed to find what I am about to say written into a policy or treatment protocol, what has happened in practice would suggest that this symptom constellation (i.e., fear of abandonment, impulsive acts of deliberate self-harm, etc.) becomes what I refer to as the clinical pertinent-positive sign signaling the need for isolation-as-treatment protocol. Ironically, the hospital acts in accordance with or in lieu of their superego. These youth also often feel like they are the family blemish not worthy of treatment, and so the isolation, in some ways, is a fitting, unconscious manifestation of their own self-loathing.

But the institutional reach of isolation goes beyond confining youth. The intentional act of youth inciting pain through countless cuts to the body as a way of diverting emotional distress into what is felt to be a deserving physical punishment is understandably difficult for any parent to accept or manage. The downstream effects create a self-esteem graveyard for parents who, in their angry or devastated helplessness, watch a kind of juvenile self-destruction that is mind-boggling to be in the presence of. They too are in a kind of traumatic isolation where, by virtue of having their child or youth taken away from them and placed into a hospital precisely because of the self-harm, it is either explicitly or implicitly understood as the job of the mental health ward to fix this wild display of developmental senselessness before a successful return to the family system. However, the teens have minds that are often far more resistant to being convinced of their cure than the hospital people or the hospital systems can handle. It is nearly impossible to cajole youth into saying that they are no longer suicidal and no longer cutting themselves — a sign of safety that would allow the hospital to discharge them into the care of anxious parents already convinced of impending failure in keeping their child safe. In other words, it is nearly impossible to achieve a cure.

While recently on call, I overheard a staff person talking about putting a patient I had just admitted on "Phase 1." I was unfamiliar with this term and was told that any youth who presented with the symptoms I have described above were to be kept in their rooms and given paper handouts to inspire emotional skill development. The intention was to get the youth to commit to staying alive and also commit to attending therapy that would be offered to them at the time of discharge. In this situation, the supervision scheme of isolation is very compelling in its cure. No big forbidding body is needed to stand over the youth to scare them into curative behaviors. The youth will be tactically situated to orchestrate their own escape through admissions of cure or betterment. Here, the isolation is more intolerable than the sickness.

On a side note, for many youths we were right to build the inpatient ward but perhaps for the wrong reasons. From the youth's perspective, at least as it has been relayed to me in post-discharge interviews, the hospital stay has been an opportunity to see others like themselves in an otherwise lonely experience. Youth have told me that the depth of their illness resulted in a belief about them being so broken that they were resistant to treatment. However, being in the hospital and being around others who similarly struggled transformed the belief that they too could not be fixed, which coalesced into an unlikely adolescent resistance fueling the beginnings of their recovery. These youth could then aggress against the idea of the adolescent ward instead of their own minds. They echoed Barbara Taylor's (2015) experience, described in her memoir *The*

Last Asylum. Taylor lived in a psychiatric asylum, a place she found deeply containing and orienting in an otherwise chaotic world that would predictably incite a chronic unravelling for her. The closing of the institution was distressing to her, which subsequently led to an intellectual protest in the form of her memoirs. In the same way, many of the youth I have interacted with rely on hospital walls and locked ward doors to insulate against an exteriority that is experienced as exclusionary and hostile. My patients have repeatedly told me that their memoirs from the inpatient unit have been etched into the undersides of their hospital beds and into the wall paint of the hospital unit. Somehow an unanticipated and unconventional womb space had emerged for the youth to heal each other, good enough in its structural nurturing conditions, yet not recognized as such.

Proto-Psychiatry

These contemporary observations have an eeriness about them when we return to Foucault and his lectures on psychiatric power. In his first five lectures, Foucault (2006) describes a kind of psychiatric historicity contextualizing his later work that will define the formation of a psychiatric subject. In his retrospective, he begins with a penetrating analysis of the origins of the psychiatric asylum and the practices that were effects of the asylum, simultaneously serving as a prototype of psychiatry, or "proto-psychiatry." In this progenitor to the practice of psychiatry as we know it today, the asylum (or psychiatric ward) is a central space. Foucault draws heavily on the writings of nineteenth-century psychiatrist Jean-Étienne Esquirol and re-asks the question that he believes Esquirol is posing, which is, "What is it in the hospital that cures?" (101). Foucault answers: "In the hospital, it is the hospital itself that cures. That is to say, the architectural arrangement itself, the organization of space, the way individuals are distributed in this space, the way they move around it, they way one looks or is looked at within it, all has the therapeutic value in itself. In the psychiatry of this period, the hospital is the curing machine" (101). How is it that the hospital manages to cure? Foucault (2006) offers an interesting interpretation that acts as the photographic negative to my own description of the hospital. In Foucault's proto-psychiatry, he narrates scenes of supervision in which psychiatric patients can be observed at all times, and where the psychiatrist is almost paradoxically absent. In the asylum it is the psychiatrist who will supervise the wardens (i.e., managers), who then supervise the nurses, who then instruct the janitors, and who all have a role in supervising the patient. It is a tidy, hierarchical system that no longer directly relies on the psychiatrist; the supervision itself has replaced the psychiatrist and signifies his presence and authority. Foucault says that the hospital can cure because it can function as a "panoptic apparatus" (102). It intuitively sees everything at all times through permanent visibility, central supervision, and the principle of isolation.

There are many educational dilemmas within this scene, but the one that is compelling to me has to do with the clear mismatch or conflation of foci. What can observations about the body tell us about the mind? Without intending to get stuck in rhetorical queries, the very basis of psychiatric knowledge is put into question in these scenes of supervision. A problematic of relationality between subject and cure is at hand when the psychiatrist believes he is directing treatment and yet is paradoxically absent. Psychiatry is doing or enacting because a body is there to be worked on, and at the same time is reliant on other bodies to do its work. But in this organizational schema, we are still left with pressing questions of how the mind works, how it veers off course, and how it is cured from confusions that leave patients unwell. In other words, we are no closer to a science of the mind in this historical and contemporary framework of psychiatry, leaving a kinetic chain of uncertainties in its wake.

Foucault (2006) describes an educational ground zero for me, subsequently creating an accessible bandwidth for understanding what is happening in my world. He suggests that reaching into the human body with regimes of control, order, and regularity are critically essential in the practice of psychiatry and form "the very constitution of medical knowledge, since exact observation is not possible without this discipline" (2), bringing into question the idea of psychiatric knowledge. In their reading of Foucault's historical rendering of the asylum and its relations to psychiatric knowledge, Deborah Britzman and colleagues (forthcoming) state, "In this arrangement, there was power before it functioned as knowledge and the knowledge, on the part of doctors, supervisors, wardens, and even patients, was mainly intuitive and rested on the authority of bodies." Foucault therefore is not subtle in his descriptions of a crisis of knowledge. Medical knowledge has reached a tipping point more broadly understood as a crisis of truth. This brittle moment simultaneously formed the foundation of psychiatric practice from the eighteenth century up until the early nineteenth century and, according to Foucault, was mechanized as a tool in its practice. It is no small irony that this crisis has also stimulated the work of this book for me.

The Entrance Is Too Near

Increasingly microscopic in his interrogation of what makes psychiatry intelligible, Foucault (2006) notes that knowledge tests for medical practitioners in the early nineteenth century focused on the presence of anatomical pathology. Here, medical specialties were permitted to ascribe illness in the form of a "localized lesion within the organism and identifiable in the body" (265). This "made it possible to constitute clusters of signs from which the differential diagnoses of diseases could be established" (265). In other words, a pathological, obviously sick focal point could be located and excised or targeted with treatment. Psychiatry sees a very different path in which the question of diagnosis is rendered feckless when the body is absent in its diagnostic utility (i.e., there is no obvious body lesion that counts as pathology) but yet the body is essential in maintaining the case for the psychiatric asylum. In psychiatry, it is easy to see here how Foucault relies on the use of the body that, through its ability to use the senses, can fulfill the criteria to be understood as diagnostics. Once the body is present as the site for diagnostics that tautologically speaks to the questions of diagnostic inquiry, psychiatry is seen to be working with observable illness. In other words, because the body and its bodily functions can respond to questions about psychiatric illness, the body therefore has the potential to be associated with or contain psychiatric illness. Foucault then further reduces the practice of psychiatric inquiry into a clinical binary such that the pressing question is simply whether or not the patient is mad, notwithstanding the superfluous nature of the body. These skeletal elements, Foucault argues, constitute a historical interruption where "in psychiatry, the essential moment that punctuates, organizes, and at the same time distributes this field of disciplinary power I have been speaking about, is this test of reality, which has a double meaning" (268).

Foucault circles back to his original crisis dramatized by the search for truth in psychiatry now recalibrated as the search to create psychiatric subjects on the question of madness and reality. According to Foucault, the request to adjudicate the question of madness constitutes the power of the psychiatrist. This test of reality, broadly taken up as the ongoing creation of a patient subject that saturates the practice of psychiatry, acts to simultaneously confirm the diagnosis of madness and constitute disciplinary authority. Psychiatric sickness follows a path. Foucault (2006) gets to the heart of the matter by stating, "Consequently, we can say that the psychiatric test is an endless test of admittance into hospital. Why is it that one cannot leave the asylum? One cannot leave the asylum not because the exit is far away, but because the entrance is too near" (269). Foucault's observations left me wondering if I had ever encountered a patient who was referred to psychiatry and who was not deemed unwell, according to my professional opinion. And what would this signal educationally? My queries, clinical and educational, about the possibility of a patient becoming unwell precisely because of their patient status can be answered by a story that underscores the notion of an entrance being too near and the endless psychiatric questioning that constitutes judgment as authority.

The answer to my query begins with a story about one of my on-call experiences. I was asked to see a nine-year-old girl who had been admitted to our inpatient unit after waiting several days to be transferred to our facility, because she was determined to be a physical risk to herself and others. She was unable to leave, even if she demanded it. How was knowledge about this nine-year-old generated and interpreted in a way that turned so very sour? In thinking about the kinds of risk a nine-year-old can pose, the words that were said and, more importantly, the words that were resisted must be left to the imagination. Her risk was unclear to me other than my reading of her chart, which indicated that this was not the first time that she had been dissatisfied to the point of becoming aggressive. I met with her and we spoke for a long time about her recent troubles. She had supposedly become violent in her classroom, causing the kind of uproar that was immediately relegated to the status of a crisis, which signaled more broadly to her educators the possibility of a mental health breakdown. When I asked her about what had transpired, she calmly articulated, with a convincing sense of clarity, that she had wanted to do her classroom project on the history of Black people and how they had been enslaved. As a Black person in a predominantly white world, she felt that this was an important topic for her. However, this topic was not for the picking and she was told that she could not do the project of her choice. She said to me in simple terms, "I was mad and I let them know."

Indeed. I asked her if anyone had understood her anger as both legitimate and important after being told "no" to her curiosity about her own history and her own identity. Our conversation moved from this point and progressed with no sign of abnormality or emotional dysregulation. However, the emergency had already taken place. The possibility of an interpretive play on her words "I was mad and I let them know" is almost ominous in its proximity to Foucault's historical observations about madness rendered contemporary. I realized that, while there was no test to declare her "well," there was evidence easily available to the contrary. In the face of abnormality, the interview mattered less than the bodily outburst that easily found its way to the opening of the hospital. As Foucault (2006) tells us, "Abnormality is the individual condition of possibility of madness; it is what must be established in order to show that what one is treating, that what one is dealing with, and what precisely one wants to show are symptoms of madness, if really of a pathological order. For the different elements constituting the object or motive for the demand for confinement to be transformed into pathological symptoms, these elements must be set within this general web of abnormality" (272). It was clear to me that the entrance was too near for this nine-year-old, where the question posed about her behavior provided sufficient conditions to convert observations into a constellation of pathological symptoms and unnecessary diagnoses. I am not suggesting that aggression is a typical or effective response in her situation. Rather, I am bringing into focus the conflation of the notion of the atypical with abnormality, and how the discourse of abnormality in the psychiatric setting constitutes the "web of abnormality" described by Foucault. Once established, Foucault's web of abnormality is not easily dissuaded. The evidence of the girl's pathology was present in her classroom. Her state of abnormality had been deemed so by her school and the local emergency department, despite the fact that she had waited calmly wait for days to be transferred to a tertiary care setting. Perhaps this is a fitting case to use as an exemplar in thinking about what it signals as an educational problem and how this moves us toward questions of meaning in education. I wonder what the nine-year-old made of her experience. She may have arrived at an understanding that school was not a place to help her understand, teachers were not there to help her question and learn, and that the real curriculum had to do with conforming. Newness in the form of possibility, exploration, and creativity was not permitted. Instead, she likely came to recognize that her acting out signaled her *as* the problem, as opposed to enacting a problem having to do with meaning. However, the acting out became the crisis, preventing others from recognizing the real crisis of exclusion that was at hand for the nine-year-old.

In my thinking about education, there is also a parallel and a paradox to be found. How should we involve education when education itself is frequently oriented toward emergency and its own crisis of natality and matricide? In the case descriptions above, how can we think about education without the thought of education itself becoming a crisis? Returning to Britzman's (2021) suggestion that education is not what happens but rather the meaning that we attribute to what has happened, a question emerges about the very purpose of education. Does education have a mandate for understanding? If so, what are we to understand? In the scenario I described, the work of understanding as an educational mandate runs the risk of being swept up in the urgency of a crisis that simultaneously signals a space for the language of abnormality. Language then can act as a defense against understanding or can foreclose on it, leading the learner into a dead end in trying to make sense of it all. In revisiting these interpretations, we also are returning to the original idea of authority in psychiatry that itself acts as a form of judgment: coming to authoritative conclusions. Educational iatrogenics are also at play in that we are left with a metaphorical "dead end," suggesting that a new educational problem has been created as a side effect of the original crisis. The dead end is the problem of the entrance to the asylum being too near, suggesting that illness is waiting to be constituted.

I want to take Foucault's example of the "entrance being too near" one step further in its metaphoric relevance. While it was not difficult to think about scenarios in which the institutional entrance was too easily accessible, the opposite has also been true, in my experience. I have found that the entrance was shut tight when it was needed. Youth whom I have been providing care for will, at times, become aware of therapeutic services that are being offered by the various mental health programs in our community and indicate a desire to participate. Typically, their rationale is well thought out and bears a kind of maturity, suggesting that they understand the hospital encounter (i.e., inpatient or outpatient) as part of the way forward in relieving their suffering. Many of them have spent time on psychiatric inpatient wards or have worked with other mental health clinicians, and so come to this conclusion with experiential knowledge such that they prioritize the opportunity for progress over emotional discomfort. Often, being admitted to the hospital or a treatment program creates a temporary "sick role" that is coupled with an expectation of recovery that they cannot yet muster. And yet when I have attempted to arrange admissions or transfers to various services within the hospital or the community, the door will not open. The youth is deemed either too sick, or not sick enough, or does not have the "right kind" of illness, or the youth appears "too eager" to be a part of treatment, inciting a kind of paranoia about the kinds of nefarious intent that could be fueling the youth's motivation.

The *too-near-nature* of the entrance signals two problems so far. Either the doors indiscriminately swing wide, welcoming all, or are tightly shut, resistant to those who may need entrance. Whether the problem is about questionable admittance or denial of admittance, a diabolically ambivalent dilemma nothing short of a crisis has been created. At the heart of the matter is the fact that the mind and knowledge of its workings still remain elusive to psychiatry, no matter if the door is wide open or closed tightly. This very conflict also speaks to the emotional situation of psychiatric education in which those learning within it, like me, are also affected by it. I am also intimately aware of how much of this conflicted drama depends on the exchange of language: perceptions of what is being said, misunderstandings about what is not said, critical omissions, awkward silences, words stumbled over, and moments felt. In recognizing these vulnerable vicissitudes constituting the psychiatric interview, I will now turn to the act of interviewing in psychiatry as a conduit for knowledge and its breakdowns.

The Psychiatric Interview: Foucault's Heredity and Melville's "Bartleby the Scrivener"

Foucault (2006) preoccupied himself with specific modes of psychiatric testing, including psychiatric questioning, otherwise known as the psychiatric interview. Here the physical body is paradoxically absent in its diagnostic utility. As far as Foucault is concerned, a grand ploy is set up in the act of taking a medical history, where a search for family pathology is liberated and ultimately successful in determining a historical chain of significations that would sanction the notion of madness as a medical origin: "Heredity is a way of giving body to the illness at the very moment that this illness cannot be situated at the level of the individual body; so, one invents, once cuts out a sort of huge fantastical body of the family affected by a mass of illnesses. . . . Trying to trace heredity therefore means substituting a different body and correlative material for the body of pathological anatomy; it constitutes a meta-individual *analogon* of the doctor's organism" (271). Within this heredity, the body acts to condemn itself in that its presence will be sufficient as a substitute for any lack of symptoms rather than an absence of pathological anatomy that can be excised and held up to account for disease. In this scene, psychiatric questioning constitutes the progenitor to abnormality. It is as if the psychiatric interview says, "The patient's body, present for the interview, will likely be sufficient in my search for disease. If I can't find pathology in the patient, I will find it in the family." There is a density of forces at play leaving the patient unaware of the vectors acting upon them. How the mind and its working can be understood as pathological or abnormal is a tactical function of the psychiatric interview, but the question really has to do with who has the upper hand in this encounter.

In my training of psychiatry, the review of the family history is often looked to as a litmus test of sorts, referred to during an encounter with a patient who does not, or cannot, or refuses to provide symptoms that are compelling enough to warrant diagnostic certainty. But the problem, as Foucault has pointed out, is that the psychiatric door is too near.

Many of my adolescent patients disengage but stay put in the interview when it would otherwise be obvious that a suspension or ending had occurred. In the adolescent failure to depart and failure to speak, he or she has inadvertently made clear a tacit infrastructure that is the psychiatric interview. In other words, the patient must speak. However, many of my patients have responded (or not) in the way that Herman Melville made famous in *Bartleby the Scrivener* (1995). That is, Bartleby refused to speak by answering all questions with the utterance "I prefer not to." Melville's short story invites us to consider the meaning of silence *as* an interview: What happens when we can't get to the question? A world is created where the primary object of a seemingly vapid Bartleby (or patient) demands an emotional subject in the life of the physician, forcing the spotlight onto the one who interviews. Bartleby's narrator (or I myself in the role of the interviewing psychiatrist) then must embark on a transference journey in which the affective vectors of frustration, defeat, madness, compassion, tolerance, identification, admiration, and perhaps the notion of love emerge around the irresolute silence of Bartleby.

I too have experienced the compulsion to repeat, questioning endlessly in the face of adolescent mutism, believing with an evangelical fervor that if the right question is posed in just the right way at the exact right moment, a magical opening will be discovered and truth revealed. Or rather, illness as a form of truth will be discovered. But according to Foucault's historical interpretation, the silence is less of a problem than the possibility of madness that lurks. A major fault line now appears.

The ontological crack is the silence that is Bartleby (vis-à-vis my adolescent patients). His character is presumed to have no navel or umbilical cord connecting him to any sign of hereditary illness, leaving the psychiatrist's work frustrated and unintelligible. This exemplar finds its way into Foucault's observations where heredity links the patient to madness in a way that defends against a meaningless situation for the psychiatrist. Meaninglessness, in this context, is the inability for the psychiatrist to locate pathology.

The physician in this scenario is made as lifeless as a silent Bartleby or as mad as the possibility of patient abnormality. Paralysis and madness seemingly become the limits that, if reached, will tether psychiatrists to illness. Psychodynamically speaking, the doctor's fears surface in the slippery slope of transference about the mind. Herein lies the potential scandal in psychiatry: is the doctor as sick as the sickness itself?

Uncertainties of the Human Profession

In offering the story of Bartleby, I am not suggesting that psychiatrists are sick and therefore should not practice psychiatry, nor I am suggesting that we should do away with the psychiatric interview. Rather, I am returning to the iterative ways in which a profession that is seemingly predicated on the healing of the mind discursively finds itself at odds with its institutional mandate, thereby facilitating its own confusion. My observations also are placed in contrast to modes of medical practice taken up by Sacks as he attempts to create connection and coherence within a generative relationality that would, over time, bring clarity for him. I can see a number of different reasons for the institutional disorientation described by Foucault, all of which come to bear on the question, Why have psychiatry? In posing this question, it stands to reason that psychiatry itself is not an inanimate force that can act upon patients, thereby demanding a body to take on the role of a psychiatrist. However, Foucault (2006) argued that the architecture of the asylum and its aspirations took on a kind of authoritative power, resulting in actions upon actions that functioned as if they were doing the work of psychiatry. Foucault states, "Psychiatric power is above all a certain way of managing, of administering, before being a cure of therapeutic intervention: it is a regime" (173). What then does the psychiatrist do? According to Foucault, "The Psychiatrist is someone who directs the operations of the hospital and who directs individuals. Just to indicate not only its existence, but also the clear awareness of this practice on the part of psychiatrists themselves" (174). In the absence of the psychiatrist's presence, and without a patient's body to orient the discourse, knowledge about illness then acts as a substitute for reality, leaving one with only the mind as a problem with unsatisfactory solutions. And if the psychiatrist is removed, the scenes of supervision remain to provide an account of the patient, an account that exists as its own form of knowledge about mental illness. Foucault suggests that, in doing so, the psychiatrist renders himself as mad as the patients. At this point, it is reasonable to step back and ask, Why then have psychiatrists when the scenes of supervising in hospitals will do? And if your patients don't speak to you but you can rely on heredity as a form of diagnostic confirmation, why have psychiatry?

Tragic Conclusions

Psychiatric signs and symptoms may have changed over time, but the biological framework of psychiatry continues to signal an education that relies on bodies to act and to be acted upon in the absence of making sense of the mind, reinforcing a concealed tautology at play. Because the psychiatrist says you are ill, so it is, thereby removing the psychiatrist from his or her knowledge and rather positioning the knowledge of psychiatry as a knowledge that cannot affect the knower. And perhaps here I want to pause and point out what I see as the real tragedy of the hospital people. There is a pretense of knowledge of the other. While I am not suggesting that psychiatric expertise is not credible nor that administrative oversight is not valuable, a vulnerability within the hospital remains as it relates to presumptions of knowledge. Foucault's thinking, albeit predicated on historical observations, has opened to a real contemporary possibility in which psychiatric knowledge is a philosophical misnomer, relying instead on a penchant for family history, body, and the power that is the psychiatrist to create a subject through these unlikely vectors of illness. If psychiatric knowledge is to engage the work of knowing the other, a counterpoint to this static endpoint is needed to open the possibility of an intersubjective encounter.

As I conclude this chapter, I want to briefly introduce the work of Koichi Togashi (2020), a Japanese psychoanalyst who offers me a nontraditional compass to work my way out of the hospital people tragedy. Togashi suggests a reconfigured space where people meet without roles or knowledge or presumptions of each other, leaving behind certainty in favor of a shared human emptiness that is the "zero" moment. Togashi's work and its influence on my attempts at an educational "ground zero" will bring me to chapter 5, where I work and practice academic psychiatry in an African context. Whether I leave the hospital at home or arrive in Africa, I am trying to convey a sense of being pressed upon by the imperative of moving toward a truly intersubjective educational field that can not only tolerate the very human uncertainties inherent in the epistemological exploration of a theory of mind but can also thrive as an effect of accepting the uncertainty.

Five

Clinical Encounters
of a Close Kind

It is easy to see how, in my discussions so far, dualities marked by mind versus body, male versus female, physician versus patient, and knowledge versus knower are prominent themes that have helped me articulate educational tensions but have limited staying power in moving beyond the many uncertainties that I am left grappling with. Through his psychoanalytic work, Koichi Togashi (2020) has provided not only a generative way into understanding these problems of dualities but perhaps also a transformative one. Togashi suggests that Cartesian dichotomies impetuously infiltrate and anchor Western modes of psychoanalytic thinking, inadvertently conceptualizing the dynamic of dualities and their boundaries as a cultural artifact of colonization. Togashi writes, "Surrendering ourselves to the moment without division, between certainty and uncertainty, puts us in a vulnerable position" (109). Indeed, this space is a call to *being* as humans without the organizing awareness of the many dichotomies I have spoken to. As I continue to dialogue with Togashi, another facet of surrender is described in Susan Neiman's (2024) essay on a recent biography of Frantz Fanon by Adam Shatz. Here, she agrees with Togashi's observations on the futility of thinking along lines of separation and says that we can think of Fanon's writing as "a meditation on the absurdity of racialization and as a vision of existentialist humanism that could free us from the racial and colonial histories of the past" (9). Neiman goes on to suggest that universalism, which she describes as a departure from thinking constituted by social tribalism, is a preferred and alternative mode of thought. Specifically, she embraces the view of a common human dignity organized and connected by our shared humanity. She says, "It takes an act of abstraction to become a universalist; to see the possibilities of common dignity in all the weird and gorgeous ways human beings differ" (11).

Indeed, her comments suggest an alignment with Togashi's departure from dualism but also bring a depth of richness in her suggestions of a welcome experience of not knowing or an alienation that paradoxically does not alienate in our commitment to finding each other and responding in kind. Neiman's description can be directly, if not concretely, applied to the possibility of imagining medicine abstracted as an antidote to the educational tribalism that medical culture insists on. Togashi has more to say on this and articulates an awakening to the possibility of suspending interpretation, diagnostics, pathology, or unmet needs in favor of an intersubjective and relational framework that can, in its capacity, tolerate the not knowing and perhaps offer something I had never previously imagined. It is this space of aesthetic void that I am referring to as a type of decolonizing learning, a working toward shedding of certainty that resembles unlearning.

In the same way that I could not name what I was learning while I was learning it, I can now look back and say that this curriculum of negative capability Togashi speaks of was deeply present for me during my time of learning, practicing, and teaching psychiatry away from home. From my experiences as a medical student in Uganda to eventually being on faculty in a Ugandan university, vulnerability was not forced but rather readily accepted by me to engage a context very different from my own. The idea of going to another setting with the recognition that confidence would and should evade me translated into a forced position of working toward epistemic humility. I felt that this type of learning stance was imperative for me to be able to consider working in Uganda. This space of affecting uncertainty, which interestingly did not feel anathema to the work of expert knowledge, profoundly influenced my career more than any other experience. Over the past twenty years while working in Uganda, I have kept a journal. Some of its entries will be shared, interrogated, explained, retold, and used throughout this chapter as a curriculum of experiences. These experiences cohere a kind of thinking that can be read as a case of thought transformation, or, more precisely, as the case of my thought transformation. Some of the journal entries are lengthy and exemplify a process of working through. My time in Uganda permitted a space for me, as an academic physician, where the principal mode of working was primarily through a deep awareness of not knowing. My entries act as a compass pointing to the iterative discoveries of what I did not understand and how not knowing became a resource to me. Looking back, I arrived at three poles: negative capability, surrendering, and universalism, which together prop up the problem of close clinical encounters in an educational third space.

> Journal Entry
> July 2001
> Kampala, Uganda
>
> I arrive in Uganda as a third-year medical student prepared to learn about emergency medicine in this setting and to do some collaborative research. As I encounter Uganda for the first time, I am struck by a resource setting comparatively very different to the one where I study. This awareness initially registers for me as guilty inequities. I feel like the experience of being here compels me to interrogate my own assumptions, if only to make sense of what I don't want to admit I am unsettled by. At

times, egregious resource disparities in medicine translate literally into life-and-death matters. In the Ugandan hospital where
I work, I have witnessed firsthand that the reality belonging to
the have-not's is sometimes a death sentence when it comes to
healthcare. Nothing in any of my educational experiences so
far has pressed upon me so intensely. And despite this being a
mostly unsettling experience, I also feel a penetrating aliveness
to learning and in doing so, feel alive to myself as a learner in a
way that has not happened before.

It was clear to me that the connection between my experience in Uganda
and the idea of learning had formed a type of educational umbilical cord and
delivered something of which I wanted more. And so, I returned to Uganda as a
postgraduate trainee for half a year in 2006 as part of my formal Canadian psychiatry education. Here I trained alongside others, like me, whose goal was to
become a psychiatrist. My presence seemed unquestioned, or at least I did not
sense any animosity or feeling that I ought not be there. In fact, I was quickly
welcomed and joined a group of learners who became both friends and professional colleagues, even now. One of the Ugandan individuals who stands out
to me is Godfrey.

In 2013, I responded to an invitation from Godfrey, who had taken on the
position of chair in the Department of Psychiatry at a university in the south-
west of Uganda. He asked if an educational partnership in psychiatry postgraduate training was of interest to me. I was now on faculty at McMaster
University in the role of associate professor and training director in psychiatry
and had openly declared an interest in education scholarship. Godfrey asked if
we could we bring our learners and faculty together to share expert psychiatry
knowledge and skills in his postgraduate training program. I could only articulate the moment as too good to be true because it allowed me an opportunity to
return to meaningful relationships in Uganda, both professional and personal.
But his invitation also offered an opportunity to return to a context that I had
experienced as possessing an uncanny educational heft, and at the same time I
could not really articulate why or how or what this signified.

His invitation to me also arrived at a time when I wanted an escape from my
clinical context at home. The demands for practice governance in Canada often
felt like management rhetoric to me and had become an unwelcome companion in my clinic where I was also an educator. The need to adhere to the DSM
and its diagnostic criteria resulted in a mental heaviness that compressed my
practice into what felt like a one-dimensional transaction that left no one satisfied. Losing its shadow was nearly impossible in a milieu obsessed with quality improvement. Contextual constraints like these had begun to wear at me.
Did Godfrey's offer legitimate my desire to escape? Was I happy to have more
than tourism as a motive for traveling to Uganda? Could I wonder, out loud, if
going to Uganda and participating in the educational partnership might obviate

my clinical load and its associated cognitive burdens, giving me a clandestine reprieve from the relentlessness of clinical care?

Albert Memmi (1992) suggests that the colonizer is one who is on a "voyage towards an easier life" (3) that eventually results in an understanding benefiting from a new status. He asks, "For how long could he fail to see the misery of the colonized and the relation of that misery to his own comfort? He realizes that this easy profit is so great only because it is wrested from others. In short, he finds two things in one he discovers the existence of the colonizer as he discovers his own privilege" (7). I knew that it wasn't an easier life that I wanted; however, I knew that a meaningful life was desired, and perhaps Memmi was onto something as it related to my motive and my wishes. In my clinical educator work at home, I found it increasingly difficult to think, whether it be creatively, critically, generatively, or at all. I knew that I could not make sense of what I only felt as a sense of being without or lacking. It was as though my knowledge, clinical interviews, interventions, or educational engagement was deficient. And lack as a resource seemed to me to be deeply problematic as a motivation to go to Uganda. What I most anticipated is that Godfrey's invitation could open for me novel modes of thinking about education in the Canadian psychiatry context. I was not entirely a stranger to what psychiatry entailed in Uganda, but I was aware that each encounter I did have in Uganda forced a welcome reconsideration of what I thought I knew. I offer the following case in which I was a clinical supervisor to Canadian psychiatry trainees I accompanied to Uganda to participate in the educational exchange with Godfrey and his trainees as an example of coming to these observations. Just before I share the next journals, it may be helpful to know what I thought was going to happen or what I anticipated I was entering into as a clinician educator in Uganda. Although I had been to Uganda many times previously, I had limited experience with the responsibilities of a clinician educator who was now a part of the faculty and who would be responsible to learners from both Canada and Uganda. I had several anxieties and fears prior to the trip. I feared that I would revert to relying on reductionistic, binary thinking and view clinical encounters through a type of moral compass, anticipating that psychiatric practice would be dramatically different in Uganda and therefore necessarily wrong. A deeply engrained habit for me was the deficiency dialogue, which I worried would readily return to shine its light on problems where my job as both teacher and clinician was to provide some meaningful interrogations or interpretations. I hated the idea that my teaching might exclusively take the form of a critique of the different aspects of psychiatric practice in Uganda. Or worse, I feared that I would return to my own practice in Canada as the exemplar of psychiatric expertise. If this was the only way I knew how to practice or teach psychiatry, how could I possibly inspire learners to experience psychiatry, or learn psychiatry, as a place of possibility? How could I be an expert in anything other than critique or a myopic veneration of what I already knew? The guile and panic of this fantastical anticipation was breathtaking. But before I get ahead of myself, I will let the journals tell you what actually happened.

Journal Entry
September 2018
Mbarara, Uganda
Arriving at Questions of Understanding: The Case of the Blue Chairs

We arrive in Mbarara in early September 2018. I am accompanying and supervising two Canadian senior psychiatry trainees in Uganda. We have spent months with a preparation that I have little faith in. We start our experience in Uganda by participating in hospital department rounds; a time dedicated to reviewing all inpatients, their problems, and their progress. Patients typically stand and form protracted lines well in advance of the workday's start. Despite the numbers, seats are few and enact a disparaging inequity registering as a familiar condition articulated in the psychiatric interviews that will continue long past the workday's end. Patients are in differing states of mind in this lineup to see the doctor. There are some that are very unwell and whose caregivers work in desperation to manage the nakedness, the intrusiveness, the screaming, and the noncompliance while at the same time trying to secure a position in the queue. No seating space is unaccounted for, and most stand in anticipation of meeting the doctor. In this simple status, a hierarchy exists — those who have a seat to wait in and those whose seat never existed. In the sitting arrangements for major ward rounds, another hierarchy is declared in accessing any sliver of space that can be found. It is a cast of thousands that come together to hear deeply private stories of the psychiatric patient and the illness encounter. The numbers of professional learners and trainees easily exceed thirty: students, staff, patients, and the occasional curious passerby who wanders into this scene. The consulting psychiatrist sits behind a large, roughly made table, historically created to segregate patients from staff and to architecturally signal the various positions suggested by the setting. But the table doesn't offer enough edges to insist on separation. People spill around the table such that a halo of humanity forms, oblivious to the structural demand for a separation. The lines of human proximity cannot be avoided and touch is inevitable.

Buttocks are used as insistent maneuvering agents to create an opening on already overcrowded benches. This is a pressing issue indeed. I look to my students, who are accustomed to having their own closed offices and privacy unquestioned. I suspect that the negotiation for a seat is at the bottom of their list of expectations for this trip. Now, as we all sit squeezed against each other, imitating the patient queues that await us, intimacy opens to a different kind of learning. No one appears uncomfortable with the close quarters, except perhaps for the Canadians. They lean in and whisper to me about the observed lack of privacy and confidentiality. "This would never happen in a Canadian setting," they say. And while Godfrey too has lamented the physical space and its problematic effects on patient confidentiality, I wonder if this constellation somatically and affectively staves off threats of profound isolation that inevitably penetrate when mental illness hijacks the mind and the social collections of those involved. I have been deeply touched, as I suspect the learners have as well, with the ensuing experience of humanity in the bodily architecture of patients and professionals enacting a culture of caring. It is a beautiful and poignant affront to my Canadian sensibilities, notwithstanding the effects on confidentiality.

In the midst of the rounds, one of the senior Ugandan faculty wishes out loud for fifty individual plastic chairs as a solution to this problem. Patients and hospital staff could have a place to sit. He remarks that this would certainly set their department apart from others in its opulence. If only. But the department budget with empty coffers cannot support this request. In private, I casually ask about the price of a plastic chair and the next day Godfrey and I are stuffing fifty new, neatly stacked, cobalt blue chairs into his vehicle. He has already arranged for a service man to come and etch the place of belonging into the backs of the chairs, lest anyone consider walking off with department goods. Pulling into the department parking lot leads to an awareness that our arrival was somehow anticipated. Or perhaps I want to believe this. A small but diverse group awaits the work of ushering the stacks of novelty into the department. The hands that help include the cleaner's four-year-old daughter, a patient's eighty-year-old grandfather, and a forty-five-year-old husband and father recovering from bipolar affective disorder, who shuffles and drools from the side effects of his medications as he walks. There is almost no verbal exchange explaining the task at hand. The chairs are carried with perceived purpose and, perhaps, respect for the task. Soon more patients are engaged in the lineup carrying chairs; it is striking to me that these contributions were neither requested nor formally acknowledged. No one complains. No one asks what we are doing. In fact, all are smiling as they go about carrying. As I watch, I suspect that no one knows what the chairs are intended for or how the newness will benefit any of the bodies that participate in the labour of bringing them to a place where ownership evades many. And while I feel deeply satisfied about being included in this collective effort, at the same time I wonder if the event signifies something educational for me.

Looking back on this entry, I now notice that we all carry these material objects intended to make subjective space where it has not existed: that is, a space for being, for belonging, and, perhaps most importantly, for thinking. The work of carrying these chairs has denoted for me a kind of symbolic educational need; I don't quite know how to think about education, particularly in my role as faculty in this Ugandan university, other than to see my own experience leading to this moment as being insufficient to prepare me as an educator. But holding onto the edges of the blue chairs somatically registered a type of newness, a thinking banister that has oriented me to essential questions of what it means to be a psychiatry educator and how learning to be one is shaped by disorientation to it. These questions have not existed for me until now.

It's All Out on the Table: Empty Resources

Questioning what resources are available to do the job as a physician educator is neither particularly uncommon nor all that interesting. A mundane mental list of necessary objects is easily generated: stethoscope, reflex hammer, and some sort of electronic device that will connect me to Dr. Google if the Internet is available. Perhaps for some educators, the need for pen and paper comes to mind (this depends, of course, on how old-school the educator is). But for the psychiatrist, the list of tools is relatively sparse, so to speak. What the psychiatry educator needs comes down to one important resource for me: my mind and its ability to recognize the working of others' minds, particularly when my own is not especially cooperative. I share the following scene from one of my trips to Uganda as a clinician educator.

> Journal Entry
> June 2015
> Mbarara, Uganda
>
> In the dining room of the Ugandan guesthouse where I have stayed over the years, the open-air windows surround an alcove where a few crudely made wooden tables and chairs are positioned and where the sounds of fluttering banana leaves accompany the guests. One morning, I enter the dining room to see that there is only one large table set in the dining alcove. The smaller tables where I have previously settled are no longer there. I then realize that a large tablecloth covers all of the separate tables, which have been pushed together, uneven in its collective surface. The place settings suggest that a crowd is anticipated. I make an assumption about belonging in this morning's seating arrangement and conclude that I don't. This suits me just fine and so I look for another place to sit. Successful in my pursuit, I sit down at a small coffee table in another room with no place setting. I get up to ask the server about cutlery

> and dishes, volunteering to get my own, recognizing that the one waitress is tending to a large crowd. Her stress is palpable, and I am happy to lend a hand. The server is flustered and says, "They are all on the table, madam" nodding towards the collection of dishes at the pushed-together tables. "The dishes are finished." It's all on the table, literally and figuratively. There is no more dinnerware, no storage, no hidden stash, and no special serving dishes for when additional guests come.

The educational problem as I see it, and have experienced many times before, mimics the encounter with limited resources. As an initiation to my day of teaching psychiatry in Uganda, where I feel that there are many expectations to fill human resource gaps that are no fault of anyone in particular, I find myself wondering what happens if my limits too are reached? The need for knowledge, insight, compassion, judgment, creativity, and stamina come to mind as the resources that I rely on to do my work as a psychiatry educator. But what if my stores are empty? More specifically, what if I have found an impasse in the form of my mind as a resource? Interpreting this scene psychodynamically opens to the possibility of my limited resources being read as an anxious introjection mimicking the inanimate properties within the dining room. To be clear, the expectations placed upon me as an educator are not introjected. I have been told explicitly by Godfrey that my role is to teach, share expertise, supervise residents, and see patients as a way of filling the educational gaps while visiting the university hospital setting as a guest faculty member. But the unconscious adaptation of my mind attentive to an empty table is perhaps less to do with the concrete educational issue of specific curricular resources than with a kind of working through to arrive at an understanding of myself as a learning resource in relationship to the questions that I have about being an educator. And this requires memory in which my interpretation of the work that I do passes through the history of my own education.

As it turns out, the problem of limited resources and its personal meaning offered up memories for me about medicine. I recall being in my last year of medical school and things turning really sour for me. I have always struggled with multiple choice questions, having relied primarily on my ability to perform music for most of my postsecondary testing. At least this is what I told myself or wanted to believe. In any event, I got three consecutive "red flags" on tests that were given to our medical school class to ensure we were all on track. I was in trouble. Or, more appropriately put, I was trouble. I got a letter indicating that I would be asked to see an educational advisor to guide my progress and to provide support in order to help me be a successful student. This support person turned out to be a middle-aged euphemism seemingly unimpressed with the perceived ineptitude that sat in front of him. In short order, he told me I did not have what it took to be a physician and that I should strongly consider leaving medicine. End of story. Not once did he ask if there was anything going on in my life that might leave me not at my best. I did not tell him that my marriage, like many other partnerships struggling with the demands of medicine, was unravelling. I did not tell him that I was trying to put together a life as a physician, which I loved so far, while another part of my life was falling apart. Instead, I told him that I was capable of being a physician and that I would do the work needed and that I would be successful. His sneer suggested that his real work had to do with cleansing the medical profession of the naive incompetence I represented.

To me, a tragedy occurred in his empty utterance. I was a danger to medicine, in the same way that Oliver Sacks's research supervisors had described him and that had resulted in his banishment to the backwoods of patient care. As in Sacks's experience, those representing institutional leadership at the university where I trained had a mandate to invite students and their situations that would inevitably fall "outside the norm," precisely as an example of educational success and not liability. My outsider status came, in part, from a former education in music. Sacks, as I have surmised, was an outsider because he did not have success as a bench scientist, but also because of his sexual orientation and his insistence on thinking in a manner that could go beyond empiricism. The educational advisor that I speak of, whether he was aware of my "outsider status" or not, could not or would not engage the work of "setting the table" for me or for others like me who did not have a traditional science background but simultaneously had something to offer. Yet the work done by the educational advisor was unfortunately not educational work at all. The ill-informed judgment by a nonphysician male who was a literal stranger to me and knew me only as an effect of testing metrics would act on behalf of the institution and deliver an empty pronouncement about me. Reading this encounter dynamically, my fears about being of no value as an educator were remnants of an unwelcome introjection made accessible to me through the scene of the empty table.

I see now that the problem has less to do with me personally, and with my assumed uselessness in medicine, and more to do with a void and how we both experience it, educator and student, and how it helps us to think about resources in medical education. While the gentleman who made the empty pronouncement may have also been an effect of the weariness that Arendt (1993) describes, in which newness is anathema to the practice of education, and therefore received me with a beleaguered hostility, I needed to survive it nonetheless. His hostility, as Arendt predicted, enacted a sense that my newness to education was like a form of hostile invasion. But it strikes me that there was an opportunity for this gentleman to either step aside or work to overcome his hostility. It is not difficult to imagine how it is that I have emotional antennae attuned to empty spaces. However, beyond this awareness, the emptiness that occurred in the transaction enacts an opening to think deeply about it.

Emptiness

How then can emptiness help me as an educator withstand the situation with the medical advisor? In short, extricating myself as the problem so as to then identify what else might be happening helped realign my orientation to the problem itself and to myself as an educator. I have, in so many words, spoken about the educational advisor's words as an introjected illness that amputated any idea of my educational potential, which I too readily embodied until the work of coming to the table and working to set it right. Continuing on with the metaphor of amputation, it was precisely cutting myself off from his proposed ideas about me that was generative, leaving me with a new unoccupied space. Togashi (2020) speaks about the use of emptiness as therapeutic tool in his psychoanalytic work, which he aligns with Emmanuel Ghent's idea of emptiness or surrender (27). Ghent's idea of surrender embraces Eastern philosophy, where, in contrast to a Western interpretation of submission or defeat, emptiness possesses a "quality of liberation and letting go" (cited by Togashi 2020, 3).

Togashi (2020) describes his work as being mindful of Western thinking yet oriented in Eastern modalities of thought and contemplation. He explains this position as a place where "patient and analyst can recognize each other as having a shared subject yet experience each other as individual minds" (4). This position presupposes a moment that surpasses description or taxonomies and surrenders to a shared intersubjectivity where sameness and difference can be held. In my mind, this is much like the qualities of the womb, where two separate existences are related and dependent on one another. And in returning to Neiman's (2024) idea of universalism as a synonym to Togashi's description of surrender, she suggests that the emotional logic of dignity is at the core of the human exchange, with the earliest exchange also being the conditions of the womb where the struggle to survive plays out both together and individually. I needed to survive the experience with the educational advisor, but in retrospect, the advisor also needed to survive his own malice and discontent. Togashi and Neiman provide a way for us to both emerge better rather than worse off for what happened between us through a different kind of orientation.

In making observations about my story, what is it that needs letting go of and how is this interpreted as or capable of being an act of resourcefulness? Togashi (2020) says that the Western instincts are to fill the void. A commitment to the void therefore emerges as an educational idea where "freedom from any interest to control or dominate, as well as devotion to human relationships, . . . allows for creativity and development to unfold in the intersubjective field" (4). This notion of another space described as a different kind of empty would see a dismantling of medical education paradigms where aggressive projections rendering the problematic student an empty transference decoy must be dismantled with the hopes of something different, something less loaded, and the meaningful heft of emptiness more apparent.

The emptiness of the table in the Ugandan inn and how it located a signal attuning me to past pain enacted on behalf of education, led me to the very resource that I had initially equated with a threatening attack. Here I discovered that a different conceptualization — that is, departing from a personal enactment of being a problematic emptiness (i.e., identifying as a nothing or a nobody in educational medicine) to thinking generatively about emptiness and its educational potential offered surprising joyful and creative emancipation not otherwise imagined.

Phantasmagoria and a Goat: Dreams of an Educator

I return now to a trope that Sacks (2016) repeatedly animates, particularly in his memoir chapter titled "Awakenings," but never says outright: that is, speaking about the joy of not being taught but learning to teach nonetheless. Sacks is fascinated by the uniqueness that constituted each of the postencephalitic patients he encountered, rendering a way of thinking that paradoxically helped create symptomatic intelligibility out of patient observations he called "fossil behaviours" (170) — behaviors that represented unconscious reactions, undeveloped in their signification of clinical differences. He notes, "It was a syndrome that included an enormous range of disturbances occurring at every level of the nervous system, a disorder that could show far better than any how the nervous system was organized, how brain and behaviour worked at their more primitive levels." (170). He describes this phenomenon as a "phantasmagoria" (170) that infers a kind of sequential orientation of images that may be imagined or real or dreamlike in its quality. And it is in this dreamy state of mind that a question is raised: how might the dream or the dreamlike state help the teacher in its strange approximation of reality?

With this question hanging in the air, I return to a phantasmagoric scene I actually encountered in Uganda—of a goat being led to slaughter—and narrated in my journal as if it were a dream, not because it wasn't real but because its enigmatic qualities render it strikingly similar to a presumed nonsensical series reminiscent of the disorientation that frequently organized the start of my workday. Looking back, I read deep condensations of cultural conflicts in my journal entry. But for now, the following is the dreamlike data.

> Journal Entry
> December 2017
> Mbarara, Uganda
>
> I will have a full day of teaching ahead, and I must pass through the inn's small parking lot in order to make my way to the hospital. I clutch nervously at my bag, demanding insistence of its presence, with nothing in it of significance. Today a goat stands where cars would typically be. A small group

of people are gathered around it, talking, gesturing with animation. More people emerge from nowhere. A woman whom I recognize as one of the cleaners at the inn is brandishing a large, mean-looking rudimentary knife. She has dark eyeliner on. She turns to me and speaks. I am somewhat caught off guard by her acknowledgement of me. I find myself wanting to hide yet feel compelled to continue watching. She tells me she will slaughter the goat — she knows how. There is a pride in her voice that commands respect. It takes six adults who emerge seemingly from thin air to help pull the goat up a set of stairs; one takes a back leg, three at the front of the goat yank on the lead rope tied tightly around the goat's neck, another two try to push the goat's behind hoping that force will propel it where it needs to go. The silent goat will not budge. I wonder if the goat wonders about being pulled apart. Is the goat the bad guy or the hero? Or is the goat a bystander? I can't tell. The goat looks forward with a stoicism that does not betray thoughts or emotions. I can't read the goat. I find myself confused about this anticipated bloody mess happening in a parking lot. Is this what really happens when something is cleaned up? I wonder if yellow tape will be included in what feels like a crime scene not yet declared with a goat at the centre of it all.

So, what are the disorienting or maddening properties in this scene and how can they act as a topographical map in orienting the educator? In other words, how can wild thinking help me think as an educator? In my scenario, there is a weapon being brandished, someone who claims an expertise with it, and a seeming victim or potential victims. And then a lot of anxious fluttering on my part, irrespective of how I imagine myself embodied within the scene. But the rest is up for speculation. A suspension is required: a suspension of intelligibility over time that would otherwise foreclose on knowing what I cannot know, allowing the uniqueness of the situation to be exactly what it is. And only through the course of endless random encounters and benign conversations does the experience render itself obvious, which coincides with the very moment that it constitutes its own intelligibility. This understanding is similar to the way Darian Leader (2012) describes our orientation toward familiarity, and away from the unintelligible. He says that in a world increasingly oriented and even coerced to "think in uniform ways, from the nursery to the corridors of professional life" (2), attending to psychical realities that are deeply individual, such as a psychotic belief or a dream, can be a welcome surprise in the creativity that it directs us to as a form of thought. These suspensions are similarly counterintuitive to educators; the nightmare situation of being in the front of the class as a teacher but not knowing how to teach the lesson nor when it will end highlights this idea. And this orientation to thought, at once suspended, tolerating unintelligibility and the suffering that it imposes on the educator primed for the expertise of delivering a learning cure at every turn, acts now as a new form of education for the educator. Otherwise put, the problem may be aptly understood as being mad without going mad as an educator. It is the very primitive dimensions of the dream that presents its own reality in brute form; that is, we cannot argue with it because it veils its own procedures. The manifest meaning of the dream is less important than the latency of understanding that is being missed, highlighting the idea of a "missed experience" that signals an atonement to it. It is this precariousness of knowability that Sacks also understood how to hold lightly, so to speak, in his discovery of awakening among his patients that was never a phenomenon with "immediacy." I am seeing dreams, broadly applied here, as one of the antidotes to learning in which the grip on certainty loosens and offers temporal possibilities anew through stall tactics employed against the reflexive, immediate need to arrive at conclusive certainties, without getting lost in the madness of the dream. I found it through my story of a goat in Uganda.

Hospital Gates

I turn now to a memory of arriving at my place of work in Uganda and how this act of coming to something sets up the stage for a timely anticipation of what cannot be anticipated and what the meaning of time has to say about recall applied to the work of education. Up until this point, I can step back and say that my journal writing suggests a vulnerability in conveying the disorientation of knowing that what I know as a psychiatrist, mostly does not fit. But the ill-fitting extends past psychiatric facts and theory, foregrounding a personal and professional exposure in which I am the emperor and I become aware that I have no clothes on. But the nakedness does not leave me worse for wear. I can now look back and locate a weaving together from what appears to be at once strange and familiar and from a time zone that simultaneously observes past, present, and a period of waiting. Deeper thinking and more generative interpretations begin to emerge from my journals and replace the fear of harsh judgments historically relied upon to do the work of psychiatry. A slow redress toward thought transformation can be read into the following journals, doubling as an act of resistance necessary to survive education.

> Journal Entry
> November 2019
> Mbarara, Uganda
>
> Arriving at the hospital grounds in Uganda, the smell of fear, acrid and anticipatory, surrounds me. I don't need to bend my ear far to find explanations. I overhear two young people working at an open-air hospital kiosk selling soap and biscuits talking in English loudly enough that I can eavesdrop. The one insists that her colleague is not taking seriously enough the

nefarious possibilities of the hospital. "Gwe [i.e., casual use of the word *you*] — you should be fearing. They can inject you and you don't even know if they have given you poison."

Doubt about Western medicine hems the road to it. I smile with the recognition that I too am one of the doubters, acknowledging that while the source of our leeriness may be very different, the shared distrust in medicine is not groundless, to be sure. I find myself asking the same question these two kiosk dwellers are asking about the psychiatric hospital, which is, "What is actually going on in there? What happens?" Good questions with no clear or obvious answers.

Passing through the gates to the Psychiatry Department that never get locked, one response to the question "What happens in there?" is offered. I see a colleague who works as a physician's assistant and we greet each other, speaking briefly of the day's work ahead, recognizing that he will see upward of eighty patients. There is much to do, but I don't have the same kind of dread that, at times, finds me at home when there are large clinical loads and teaching duties. As we talk, a young woman comes to the sloped driveway where we stand. She is tiny and dusty, with Ugandan soil clinging to her. Perhaps she has come from the farm or the village. She kneels on her mud-soaked skirt and asks my colleague for support. I have come to understand that support typically refers to money but can really mean any number of things that in the end will result in some kind of unpossessed resource. He gently declines her request. She is so pregnant I wonder if she will deliver on the driveway. She then genuflects in front of me, her nose stretched so far over her taut belly I am certain gravity will topple her over.

A few days later, I accompany the Ugandan residents to see this very woman, now postpartum on the obstetrics ward with her limp, HIV+ newborn. She hands the sleeping infant to me, again in a kneeling position, while the residents looked on with a collective affect I found difficult to read. The mother is so very unwell and her newborn is eventually apprehended from her. It is her fourth child she has been unable to take home.

Stepping back to think about this devastating scene as an educator who is trying to locate it psychodynamically and then comment on its potential as an educational resource, I wonder about the notion of deferral and its application. There is undoubtedly much to say about the depth and complexity of this situation, in that somebody wants something, somebody needs something, and that someone has to suffer their fate. What I will or can directly comment on is the temporality of learning that presses upon me as an educator. The moment can be recalled as a story in its complex devastation, but it is also as a story that comes from behind. Possibilities of intelligibility or defense against the painful losses in this scenario collapse into a singular demand to stay with it over time. In other words, I could not tell this story before now, being frustrated in an attempt at doing so because I could encounter the story only while experiencing it through estrangement or as a fragmentation best described as an educational deferral. The psychoanalytic term *Nachträglichkeit* introduced previously orients us to that which occurs in the time of after and speaks to the work of education in this scenario that was simultaneously never there but is present only in the time of now as a deferred experience. The resource of temporality is perhaps too simplistic in its description; it is more likely the associated affect accompanying time that can be thought of as a resource. Specific to this scenario, the learning experience can be equated with frustration, and learning itself becomes a state of frustrating uncertainty that takes a temporal toll on the educator. Frustrating indeed, as the role for the educator becomes obtuse when what was needed was not only the moment but the iterative moments of the story that had no context. Herein lies the educational problem. I watched, and in doing so, joined the learners in reverting to a kind of countertransference directed toward the woman in which we acted out a historical interview that emerged earlier in this book: we took her history and asked, Is she mad or not? In pointing this out, I am not making a criticism so much as an observation about a response to the impossibility of knowing in medicine, the perceived mandate to demonstrate and to embody expert knowledge and be the leader of it. So how would deferral help me think in this scenario? This question does not have an easy answer in that the learning propensity to postpone would seemingly require time, or rather insist that I bear the burden of the story to register and coalesce, but only once the deferral has occurred. Perhaps this encounter leads me to understand that learning for the educator (and for the student) is enduring a period of gestational uncertainty in which the delivery of knowledge worth having registers after the moment is gone.

Maggots and a Sleeping Educator

I invite the reader into the next journal entry without an introduction or explanation but with the confidence that the idea of forgetting within the story will speak for itself.

Journal Entry
November 2019
Mbarara Uganda

I have entered the psychiatry ward and turn the corner towards the small nursing station that contains all of the drugs for the entire psychiatry ward in two small carboard boxes, gingerly placed upon one rusty shelf. I can smell the clinical encounter before my eyes register the event that would never otherwise be encountered in a Canadian setting. With the Ugandan residents at my side, we come upon a girl seated on the bench in an open space where patients will settle during rounds. Urine is steadily running out of her and there is a small pool underneath her, the sun glinting on its surface, unaware of what it was bringing to light. She looks down and does not speak. The head nurse tells me that the young woman has been escorted by the Obstetrics and Gynecology team and was "dumped" at the psychiatry ward. Funny, in Canada being given someone else's work is also called a dump. But it is striking here in this context how the language of inconvenience and waste is too close to home. She was not wanted on the other ward, signaling a need for a place where the outcasts go. Psychiatry is the obvious place.

The Ugandan residents immediately get to work, doing what they think needs to be done. I am not really sure what they think it is that is required but the sense of ownership and responsibility for this patient who is not theirs is remarkable and deeply moving. They quietly get gloves, shoo away the peering eyes of other patients and caregivers, politely ask for the privacy they too would desire, and kneel close enough so they can speak quietly to the mutism that is in front of them. The young woman tenses around the male residents and they are aware of her resistance. She is small, unkempt, has terrified eyes, and the smell is almost dizzying as the urine continues to leak. The female resident beside me registers an absent affect, almost shellshocked. Maybe I am projecting what I can only read as an atmospheric blank that hangs in front of all of us. I am the only faculty around at the residents who look to me. I proceed to kneel in front of her and greet her quietly in the local language. She looks frozen but utters her greeting in barely-there whispers. Speculations happen around us. How did she get to the hospital? What happened? Has she attempted an abortion and in doing so, punctured the bladder? Is she mentally unwell? I ask if she will come with me and a female resident. Can we help her? Can we examine her? She is crying. I offer her a tissue. No one else has one because tissues are a luxury item. She accepts and we go to another room. A space actually. I use the term "room" too loosely. It is the alcove at the entrance of the department where the nurses stand to give out free medications to patients who wait the length of a day for government hospital prescriptions. There is a large window opening to the public and a door that does not completely close. We have a sheepish, uncommanding divider that almost doesn't do the job of interrupting lines of vision. I am gagging from the smell. The patient says little, mostly grunts and looks away. She allows us to examine her but there is nothing much to see except the steady leak of urine. Everywhere is wet despite the sun that warms the air. We call for another nurse who speaks the patient's local language. She is tough on the girl. I read this as a response to perceived victimhood but the truth is, I am lost in arriving at any understanding. All I have is the grasp of speculation. The nurse interrogates the silent girl and I am reminded of Bartleby in her preference not to respond.

Later the nurse who speaks the patient's language comes to me and tells me that after the resident and I left the bedside, she was able to get some answers from the silent patient. I asked about the verbal encounter, curious to hear about the cadence of affecting communication, anticipating a dull agogic encounter leading to an otherwise silent exchange. The nurse is flat in her expression but reports with the slightest tinge of pride in her voice that she had said to the girl, "You will die and your insides will rot so that maggots are coming out of you and yet we don't know what has happened to you." According to the nurse's report, the fear of uncertainty easily convoluted into a threatening, pressing, lethal etiology staring down the girl's preference not to speak, and animated in her the ability to respond. She does eventually speak: she is pregnant, with syphilis, and has made an unsuccessful attempt at an abortion.

I recall what it was like to be actively in this scene as an educator; its overwhelming and simultaneously elusive qualities were felt in the silence of the patient, in the stringent, acrid scent that settled in my senses, in the blank stares of the learners, and in the rigid one-dimensional qualities of the scene, with only a series of somatic clues pointing to investigative work as a way into a problem that was yet to be determined. I too felt that my line of vision was compromised, in my inability to see clearly what was happening. But the problem was and is always a scene that works in a currency of incomplete fragments: a juggler throwing up balls in the air, each with an important, apportioned bit pertinent to the case — symptoms, pathology, diagnosis, etiology, patient care, hospital culture, gender, healthcare systems, education, trauma, alienation, and so on — and as they go up and down my instinct as an educator is to grab one to stop the dizzying pendular complexity that is in front of me, if only to steady myself. The narrative, however, is told as a coherent educational case that is precisely cohered as a deferral, similar to the case of the woman on the driveway. I wonder if the situation would have me name my own educational framework revealing itself to me in Uganda as "thinking as forgetting."

But if I step back from this scene and attempt to treat it like a transference object, opening up a new way of thinking about educational problems instead of personalizing them, this case highlights a trope of being strange, somewhat like a static position with unknown coordinates on a map. Even moving from one point to another in the story was confusing and also reads this way as it is told. Nothing made sense. Nothing seemed right. I have attempted to highlight a position in which all characters are "made strange," resorting to a state of self-alienation with a purpose. But this is not the first time I have educationally experienced or observed this affecting state in others, and its repetition signals something important for me — I am referring to an affective educational marker that psychodynamically points to the transference. Uncertainty here may be read as a kind of denial or regression to an earlier state of not knowing in which all are tongue-tied. An easy association can be made here with the scene in which Sacks relates one of his earliest accounts of journal club, a time dedicated to expert medical knowledge, but finds that he along with his fellow learners are also unable to locate language, manifesting a kind of developmental regression that is specific to education. What is there to do when there is nothing in the moment to do? Can forgetting then be a resource? Did the girl threatened with death by maggots really not recall her situation until she did? Why is it that she or anyone remembers anything painful at all? Did the learners really go blank or is this a projection on my part as a clinician educator? How can the educator who is lost be helpful in a psychical about-face where expertise has unraveled? This paradox emerging within the story is understood only as an afterthought; it is not intelligible in the moment but is provocative for educational introspection nonetheless.

Despite the knowledge and skills that surrounded this youth in the form of the team, a kind of ruthless forgetting can be read as transference, in which forgetting or silent denial is the affecting defense called upon as an articulation of difficult knowledge in a deeply traumatized learning encounter. Deborah Britzman's *A Psychoanalyst in the Classroom: On the Human Condition in Education* (2015) speaks of forgetting by describing it as an "idea that what we do not know[,] as well as what we do not want to know anything about, instructs the knowledge we thought we already had" (viii). The quality of this forgetful space is what I am interested in here. One the one hand, the story reads as a kind of educational vacancy in that no one really knew what was going on, which had the fearful effect of a "hot potato" that no one really wanted to touch. On the other hand, the scenario is alive in its painful suffering and the need for its cause to remain uncertain in order for intelligibility to have an effect as an act of deferral. If the quest to understand had been foreclosed on and premature assumptions or pronouncements made, least of all by the educator in this scene, the story would have been altered dramatically and, perhaps, for the worse. But no one did this, or perhaps could do this. Instead, those involved in the scene mostly assumed a questioning stance that demanded specificity enough to move beyond an initial ineffability to land at an articulation of "What is going on in there?" Although the embodiment of this question may not have provided an immediate answer, our bodies, and specifically my body, enacted the query through a shared encounter with the learners, the staff, and the patient in which I as the clinician educator had to rely on a space of psychodynamic forgetfulness to draw me into a closer kind of examination of this story. The authors and psychoanalysts Sally Swartz and Koichi Togashi also help me bring a new meaning to the use of affective denial or forgetting.

Swartz (2019) says of the scene of the infant and the mother, "The infant cannot use an emotionally absent or overwhelmed or terrified mother ruthlessly. Total presence is essential to survival" (8). She goes on to say, "Tolerance is too passive a word to describe the quality of survival to be summoned while being used ruthlessly. It requires putting much else aside" (7). In other words, to survive means to simultaneously forget in the moment that one is engaged in a struggle to do so. The quality of the space that is holding or tolerating the ruthlessness of uncertainty in the story needing to be transformed but not yet ready to undergo such change, otherwise described as forgetful denial, is like a generative "ground zero" in this educational scenario. Something is happening in the nothingness, but not yet declared as a point of clarity. And this holding of a slumbering educational moment may be something to think of as a generative placeholder, in wait of a rupture but not yet ready to benefit from the painful opening that is to come.

The educational situation riddled with the threat of maggots is also similar to the one described by Togashi (2020), who writes about a patient who repeatedly falls asleep during their sessions and then wakes to leave. Togashi gets anxious about the slumbering state of his client and must reckon with this unanticipated problem, relying first on the many different explanatory interpretations he generates to help him understand. These efforts turn out to be of no use to him. He concludes that surrendering to her sleep was all he could do. And in doing so, he fell into a shared, deeply human space unheeding of judgment and authority, where an unnarrated slumbering uncertainty that embodied the empty moment, even if it was a sleepy one, was essential for transformation of those in it. This, Togashi says, is also the place of an ethical turn, a place where both analyst and analysand are left empty-handed by surrendering to an emptiness that is beyond themselves, a space that exceeds the morality of right and wrong and relies on a purity inherent in human intersubjectivity. He also refers to this moment as "the psychoanalytic zero," a term uses interchangeably with the idea of an ethical turn. And to be clear, it may be reasonable to ask what is ethical about this turn, in particular for the analyst, whom we are using as an exemplar in thinking about the interactions of an educator with learners in education. Togashi suggested that with analysts, there is an awareness and an expectation that they are professionals tasked with the job of addressing suffering for the analysand. However, he is suggesting that there is a moment that predates the awareness and "asks analysts to pay attention to the ways in which they and their patients encounter each other as human beings" (29).

Coming back to the case of the girl whose death by maggots is imminently feared, but whose offering was one of silent suffering, enacted the very conditions for the educator to enter into and remain in, as much as humanly possible, and, paradoxically, it was the only possibility in that encounter. Her silent suffering could not speak, and so we had to wait with the patient and with the patient's pain for the moment of understanding to arrive. Education, as embodied by me as the educator, is sleeping. And the sleep that I speak of is not purposelessly futile but the sleep that Togashi (2020) speaks of and can be thought of as a state of present engagement for an affecting forgetfulness that fails in the moment to respond yet is as necessary as the surgical cure that will come for the young woman in need of repair. I will end with a comment that takes my own thoughts and translates them into a far more elegant statement by Swartz (2019), who suggest that the quality of ruthless forgetting I am speaking about is "common to both preservation of the original failure and subsequent thinness of concern, but also, in the right context, a reach for a new beginning" (9).

Journal Entry
June 2015
Mbarara, Uganda
Taking Tea and Survival

The common act of "taking tea" during the medical workday seems to border on the sacred, I suspect, because it marks time away from unrelenting demands that are essential to survival. For me, it serves as a sort of placeholder in the day, a pause from the incredible clinical load and associated teaching, simultaneously recognizing the impossibility of the task and the good-enough efforts that are made by all. I find that the tea break evokes in me a deep familiarity in a place that is miles away from home. I am reminded of my prairie Mennonite upbringing, a life that promotes simplicity, disavows the ostentatious, and where the everyday acts, particularly around work and eating customs, are infused with their own religious significance in an attempt to create meaning, precisely because meaning making has always silently been in question. Nonetheless, home comes to mind and I am left wondering about this thought association while I am here as an educator halfway across the globe.

During one of our afternoon teaching sessions, we talk about the importance of children. I have suggested that we "take tea" while we learn, wondering out loud about capacity for this act to "make concentration come." Concentration too has a will, as it turns out, which can be stubborn when it is hungry. The reality that I have stumbled into is the dilemma that faces many of the Ugandan psychiatry residents; that is, they also live at the edges of poverty and access to food often takes a backseat to rent demands or "airtime" for mobile phones.

We are learning about side effects of anticonvulsants which are commonly prescribed by this group to the many patients who suffer with the devastating effects of epilepsy. It is well known that these medications can reduce fertility as a potential side effect. I ask, "Who cares about sperm counts?" "I do" says one of the Ugandan male residents, without missing a beat. Everyone bursts into laughter. But it is no laughing matter. To be childless in this setting is a devastation that none can really imagine unless understood as a personal reality. A story is told by Godfrey about one of his patients; a male who has a severe intellectual disability. But the patient can get an erection and can be coached by relatives and neighbors about what to do with it. So, the patient is introduced to a woman in the community who is childless. They are married and produce two children together. According to Godfrey, the wife willingly takes on the task of changing the diapers of her infants and her husband, because this maternal role, irrespective of the incapacities of the husband, brings a respect that clearly trumps the stigma of being an unmarried, childless female. Godfrey offers this story as a clinical example of a successful psychiatric outcome.

In my narration of this educational session and leaning on psychoanalytic metonymies rendered apparent from the narrative, the thematic of survival can be read into each of the characters and the necessary intersubjectivities in the storied aliquots. Of course, I cannot speak for anyone other than myself in knowing what it was like to be there, as part of the scene. In an attempt to make psychodynamic observations about the educational scene and what it might tell me about common conflicts and resources, I stop short of making ontological or epistemological interpretations on behalf on another. But in returning to this narrative, I notice the thematic of survival and how aesthetically idealized edges contain its storied contents. A sense of home pacifies the wandering mind, hunger is satisfied, barrenness is cured, education is successful, and the psychiatrist heals. These idealities are my own and provide a sense of what is at stake in the task of surviving education and the underlying pain of encountering loss and disappointment as an educational reality. This story also thematically returns and aligns with the four main educational elements that have already been captured thus far in my Ugandan reflections: time and its delayed work, forgetting as a necessary form of affect, the void as a form of knowledge, and relying on a psychotic, dreamlike thinking as a creative antidote against cognitive ossification. While I highlight these ideas as corollaries in relationship to educational survival and what it may entail, I also am trying to make the case that there is a relationship at the heart of education that speaks to the difficulty I am trying to get at, raising the question of why survival in education matters at all and how its gendered qualities bring us back to a discourse from previous chapters.

If the idea of survival is to be any use at all to an educator, the question must be asked, When does survival become an issue for us humans? I am drawn again to the work of Swartz (2019) in considering the idea of ruthlessness in education as well as how we might think about it as a stratagem by surviving it. The concept of ruthlessness as it is understood psychoanalytically by D. W. Winnicott (2014, 265) and described by Swartz (2019) introduces a kind of therapeutic noncompliance that occurs between infants and their mother, in which infants use their mothers in the fight for their lives. Winnicott was an expert observer in interpreting these interpersonally poignant scenes between infants or children and their mothers. This dynamic struggle takes place at the breast, where hunger demands satiation from the mother at all costs in order to survive. Swartz says that ruthlessness has particular qualities: "To be ruthless is also not simply to be pitiless; in its full-throated demand, and in its expression, it embodies a vigorous act of trust. It is shamelessly naked, exposing the rawness of need as it is felt" (7).

How does the educator survive and what is it that threatens existence? In returning to the four elements suggested above — time and its delayed work, forgetting as a necessary form of affect, the void as a form of knowledge, and relying on madness as a creative antidote against cognitive ossification — it strikes me that the demand for the educator is, in part, to be the site of embodiment of these demands so that education can be made intelligible to those wanting to learn, including the educator herself. For example, being present in the above scenarios is different from being "in the moment," recognizing that time and the educational moment do not always work hand in hand, leaving the educator in wait. And while in wait, forgetting to remember and inexpertly welcoming a void as a form of educational logic emerge as educational defenses for me in attempting to understand what would otherwise might be considered mad. In other words, the educator is of use while being used alive. And here I will embrace the analogy of the mother and infant unit but render a slightly different educational interpretation, which is the intersubjective reality of the educator and the student. It is not only the educator that is surviving in this dependent arrangement but also the educational collective where the educator can be used, or even consumed, in service of education itself.

Working with Winnicott's view, Swartz (2019) also depicts the situation between analyst and analysand as one of ruthlessness:

> We want to be eaten. Patients who are able to use us ruthlessly come to therapy to feed and be fed, all in the service of reaching beyond withdrawal from or persecution by an internal world made too present by a failure to survive. Winnicott suggests that to offer ourselves for eating in this way demands that we put aside our own preoccupations and ways of experiencing time. We are being asked to dream our patients, even when their capacity to dream might be damaged. (8)

I consider this dilemma as interchangeable with education, specifically medical education. As an educator, I exist. Or at least my desire is that I am used in the service of change for learners. And this change presumably takes something from me as my body becomes a temporary site of containment where students can find a shared location in the scene of education and then then wander with imagination and authentic curiosity in attempting their own educational work. Implicit in this shared survival is an educational desire. That is, I return to the question, "What's really going on in there [i.e., teaching hospital]?" And I can answer that by returning to my own affected state, which is to register the educational claustrum as not only problems of education but life's problems as well. In recognizing this shift, I attempt new ways of intelligibility for learners through conflicts imaginatively transformed. More simply put, to arrive at the same educational problem but to see it anew, albeit in a more interesting way, is perhaps the essence of education and the meaning of surviving it.

Six

Beyond the
Empirical Divide:
A Way Out for
New Education

As I conclude, I return to the idea of surviving education and the description offered by Sally Swartz (2019) of "being used" or "being worn down" as an educator. At first glance, it seems as if I am relegated to an iterative return to the weariness suggested by Hannah Arendt (1993) when we speak of education, with no other alternatives other than to brace for what is to come. While there is little doubt that the act of wearing down translates into conflicts and questions experienced as impatient negotiations with myself, there was and also is an intense beatitude that accompanies my experience as an educator, underscoring for me what it means to be alive. Swartz (2019) comments that the pain of being present and used ruthlessly as a mother for the sake of a collective survival with both mother and infant intact "is possible because there is joy just as deep and wide and engulfing as the state of being worn thin" (8). Indeed. The wearing down may have left me weary, at times, but not worse for wear. Quite the opposite. It has led me to what Swartz describes as the aftereffects of surviving ruthlessness and the ruthless qualities of education. She notes that surviving ruthlessness as an intersubjective encounter allows for the capacity to see, with compassion, the other as uniquely and distinctly different from oneself and also, necessarily, out of our control. This freedom from omnipotence, internally or externally imposed, otherwise interpreted educationally as surrendering the fantasy of being in control or being controlled, including the subjugation of learners and learning itself, is precisely what I am suggesting allows for the quality of ruth. Swartz concludes better than I could by saying, "Ruth is compassion specifically for the other used ruthlessly in the service of survival" (8).

My memoir guide, Oliver Sacks (2016), also had conclusions to make about survival, and posited the quality of compassionate ruth precisely as survival tactics described in his own memoir chapter "Awakenings." I read Sacks's chapter as a psychoanalytic description of his personal coming alive in the same way that his postencephalitic patients did. In his awakening, he also emerged as a medical educator who has something important to say through both the prolific, storytelling brilliance of his scientific writing and also his narration of being in relationship with writing. As though Sacks was unconsciously alive to Swartz in her depiction of the intact remains of the mother-infant dyad, Sacks's ability to find life-giving reprieve through his writing necessarily included his mother. Sacks unequivocally situates his mother as central in coming to his case stories that would form *Awakenings* (1990), but also recognizes that her own skill as a storyteller, her deep interest in his narration of the authenticity of the individuality of the cases, her persistent insistence that Sacks continue to put pen to paper, and her faith in the importance of his scientific inquiry constituted the conditions of his storytelling as a form of negotiation in the pursuit of his own psychical survival and natality. Sacks recognizes the profound influence that his mother had in the writing of his book *Awakenings*. Her death occurred during this period, and in his memoir, he describes this event as "the most devastating loss of my life — the loss of the deepest and perhaps, in some sense, the realest relation of my life" (2016, 193). And here we get a glimpse into what Sacks was in pursuit of — and by this I am referring to an ongoing dynamic negotiation for an authentic, free self. The experience of losing his own mother shapes an understanding of waking up to the work of surviving education — both formal medical education, where he was largely an outsider, and surviving the conditions of life's education through increasingly tender and intimate relationalities that could tolerate the necessary pain associated with it, including a deep connection with writing in cases.

Sacks's pursuit of freedom through the work of writing also reminds us of what it means to use writing to survive ourselves as a form and force of education, and to work through places marked by guilt and pain but where a desired leniency is etched out, word by word, in the aesthetic of storytelling. Like Jonathan Rosen (2023) and his written attempts at understanding the arc and history of relationship mediated by the unspeakable weight of his friend's mental illness, perhaps a parallel central storyline appears that is his memoir. Rosen's deeply personal contemplative search to free himself from the heft of helplessness and guilt through the pardoning of writing rings true as another storyline. The threat of being broken by narration that is deeply personal and the commitment to understand what cannot be without a jettison from the haunting and unwieldy requires a different kind of repose. Rosen's careful crafting of words nurtured the out of sorts without becoming so. This is perhaps what he stumbled into. Rosen's written encounter approaches what Susan Neiman (2024) could have meant when she describes the importance of universalism: a version of the hero's journey but with a twist. Rosen (2023) wrote his own account of his friend with unfolding elements necessary for all protagonist's journeys replete with confrontations, separation, conquering, and the return — except the return signaled incompleteness for Rosen's friend Michael Laudor in his ongoing illness and incarceration. Rosen's writing, generously dedicated to understanding the precarious uncertainty that embodied everyone, permits the reader to assign a compassionate dignity to his friend's experience of illness outside of his making. When differences threaten, Rosen's writing can be expanded then to see writing itself as a survival trope.

It strikes me that I too am attempting to survive the wilderness of my thoughts, particularly in relation to my experiences of education, by writing persuasively with the hopes that something remains that is of use. I have come to understand the ways that others and I have ruthlessly engaged writing simultaneously as a survival tactic, a personal amnesty, and a compelling rhetoric in which education can be organized categorically into a complex relationship with ethos, logos, and pathos as well as ethnos and eros — all elements as case and cause for surviving life. So, can it be argued then that life's problems are also educational problems, in the way that my observations bring me to the fore of an educational discourse? Surely, humanity is subtly at stake because, as Arendt (1993) has argued, something new comes into the world. The survival of the educational situation imbued with the dynamics of life is not much different from the analysand and analyst doing the shared work of ruthless survival reminiscent of the infantile vulnerabilities at play in starting life.

Understanding, then, my own newly created space of educational problems as life problems, writing myself back into the field through autoethnographic encounters can be interpreted psychodynamically, as was Sacks's vital experience with writing. I now understand more clearly how this act of taking apart and putting back together again is like having been strange and having made strange within a medical milieu symptomatic of the educational madness etched into its history. This self-alienation undertaken with an educational purpose can otherwise be understood as the early, albeit dormant efforts of being in search of an "I." I could not see who I was or where I was until the suffering discomfort brought to light by an entrance, too near in its approximation, illuminated my positioning as a hospital person in relationship to myself. Through the process of writing into and around the narratives that have shaped educational questions predicated on the possibility of understanding, even if suspended or paradoxically made from fragments of unintelligibility, life has snuck up on me from behind and tapped me on the shoulder, pointing to a generative detour revealing alternatives to the authoritative practices made from masculine residue. Educational survival for me is really about an awakening made possible through thinking and writing in cases, delving deep into the psychiatric history that situated my extinction only to find decolonizing possibilities in which authentic engagement can occur. Like Sacks, I too have written about the many ways in which education, broadly speaking, represents the status of uncertainty demanding a ruthless survival of its opacities and resistance to voice through an orientation toward relationships enabled by my body, registered not only as an academic exclusion but also paradoxically as a gendered embodiment of the maternal potential for natality, capable of enduring a beleaguered or hostile welcome. I have settled into the fault lines where the divide between the idea of education and what has never been thought of as education has been worth the labor of interrogation because I have materialized in its wake. This ethical turn, a chasm of lost meaning precisely relying on these presumed spaces of uncertainty shared as a deeply human condition along with those patients and colleagues I learn alongside, has transcended the exclusions that now seem antiquated, and offers a point of departure to create my own understanding of education. Coming to terms with the idea that I have been the subject of time, perhaps even unwillingly, I have come to relationally experience this forgetful void as a friend whose maddening yet creative qualities have become a new authoritative antidote to submitting to and enacting the fragile ossifications that I have come to understand as education. In this act of educational resistance, I have survived myself. This kind of object relating turned into object usage with my self as the object in question has affectively illuminated a personal resource not understood until now. I am useful to myself. My self is of use. And this brings me back to Swartz (2019) and her understanding of ruthlessness according to Winnicott. She says that to be used ruthlessly "opens the way for a new form of relatedness" (7). Is this not the very definition of education? How is it that we can come to know ourselves and one another anew through the changing of our minds? While this may require maddening resources, it is, nonetheless, essential for the enlivenment at stake.

References

Arendt, Hannah. 1958. *The Human Condition*. 2nd ed. Chicago: University of Chicago Press.

Arendt, Hannah. 1993. "The Crisis in Education." In *Between Past and Future: Six Exercises in Political Thought*, 173–196. New York: Penguin Books.

Bion, Wilfred R. 1970. *Attention and Interpretation*. London: Tavistock.

Blechner, Mark J. 2005. "The Gay Harry Stack Sullivan: Interactions between His Life, Clinical Work, and Theory." *Contemporary Psychoanalysis* 41 (1): 1–19. https://doi.org/10.1080/00107530.2005.10745845.

Britzman, Deborah P. 2003a. "Five Excursions into Free Association, or Just Take the A Train." *Journal of the Canadian Association for Curriculum Studies* 1 (1): 25–37.

Britzman, Deborah P. 2003b. *Practice Makes Practice: A Critical Study of Learning to Teach*. Rev. ed. Albany: State University of New York Press.

Britzman, Deborah P. 2009. *The Very Thought of Education: Psychoanalysis and the Impossible Professions*. Albany: State University of New York Press.

Britzman, Deborah P. 2011. *Freud and Education*. New York: Routledge.

Britzman, Deborah P. 2015. *A Psychoanalyst in the Classroom: On the Human Condition in Education*. Albany: State University of New York Press.

Britzman, Deborah P. 2021. *Anticipating Education: Concepts for Imagining Pedagogy with Psychoanalysis*. Gorham, ME: Myers Education Press.

Britzman, Deborah P. 2024. *When History Returns: Psychoanalytic Quests for Humane Learning*. Albany: State University of New York Press.

Britzman, Deborah P., Aziz Guzel, and Sheila Harms. Forthcoming. "Reading Foucault's Lectures on Psychiatric Power." In *Foucauldian Philosophy and Implications for Educational Research*, edited by Denis L. Carson. New York: Routledge.

Carlat, Daniel J. 2010. *Unhinged: The Trouble with Psychiatry — A Doctor's Revelations about a Profession in Crisis*. New York: Free Press.

Cavarero, Adriana. 2000. *Relating Narratives: Storytelling and Selfhood*. New York: Routledge.

Derrida, Jacques, and Barbara Johnson. 1981. *Dissemination*. Chicago: University of Chicago Press.

Eickhoff, Friedrich-Wilhelm. 2006. "On Nachträglichkeit: The Modernity of an Old Concept." *International Journal of Psychoanalysis* 87 (6): 1453–1469. https://doi.org/10.1516/ekah-8uh6-85c4-gm22.

Felman, Shoshana. 1993. *What Does a Woman Want? Reading and Sexual Difference*. Chicago: John Hopkins University Press.

Forrester, John. 2017. *Thinking in Cases*. Cambridge: Polity Press.

Foucault, Michel. 2006. *Psychiatric Power: Lectures at the Collège de France, 1973–1974*. Edited by Jacques Lagrange. Translated by Graham Burchell. New York: Palgrave Macmillan.

Frangou, Sophia, ed. 2016. *Women in Academic Psychiatry*. New York: Springer.

Freud, Sigmund. 1964. "Analysis Terminable and Interminable." In *The Standard Edition of the Complete Psychological Works of Sigmund Freud*, vol. 23, *1937–1939*. Edited and translated by James Strachey in collaboration with Anna Freud, assisted by Alix Strachey and Alan Tyson, 209–254. First published in 1937. London: Hogarth Press.

Freud, Sigmund. 2006. *The Penguin Freud Reader*. Edited by Adam Phillips. London: Penguin Books.

Hirshbein, Laura D. 2004. "History of Women in Psychiatry." *Academic Psychiatry* 28 (4): 337–343. https://doi.org/10.1176/appi.ap.28.4.337.

Keats, John. 1988. *John Keats: The Complete Poems*. 3rd ed. Edited by John Barnard. Penguin Books.

Kitto, Simon. 2019. "'What Is an Educational Problem?' Revisited." *Journal of Continuing Education in the Health Professions* 39 (4): 223–224.

Knoll, Corina, Michael Rothfeld, and Ali Watkins. 2020. "'I Couldn't Do Anything': The Virus and an E.R. Doctor's Suicide." *New York Times*, July 11, 2020. https://www.nytimes.com/2020/07/11/nyregion/lorna-breen-suicide-coronavirus.html.

Leader, Darian. 2012. *What Is Madness?* London: Penguin Books.

Levinson, Natasha. 1997. "Teaching in the Midst of Belatedness: The Paradox of Natality in Hannah Arendt's Educational Thought." *Educational Theory* 47 (4): 435–451. https://doi.org/10.1111/j.1741-5446.1997.00435.x.

Lewiss, Resa. E., Carol A. Bernstein, Angela M. Mills, Barbara Overholser, Julie K. Silver, and Nancy D. Spector. 2020. "Is Academic Medicine Making Mid-Career Women Physicians Invisible?" *Journal of Women's Health* 29 (2): 187–192.

Melville, Herman. 1995. *Bartleby, the Scrivener: A Story of Wall-Street, 1853*. Minneapolis: Indulgence Press.

Memmi, Albert. 1992. *The Colonizer and the Colonized*. Exp. ed. Translated by Howard Greenfeld. Boston: Beacon Press.

Neiman, Susan. 2024. "Fanon the Universalist." Review of *The Rebel's Clinic: The Revolutionary Lives of Frantz Fanon*, by Adam Shatz. *New*

York Review, June 6. https://www.nybooks.com/articles/2024/06/06/fanon-the-universalist-the-rebels-clinic-shatz/.

Pitt, Alice. J. 2003. *The Play of the Personal: Psychoanalytic Narratives of Feminist Education.* New York: Peter Lang.

Pitt, Alice. 2006. "Mother Love's Education." In *Love's Return: Psychoanalytic Essays on Childhood, Teaching, and Learning*, 87–105. Edited by Gail M. Boldt, Paula M. Salvio, and Peter Maas Taubman. New York: Routledge.

Pitt, Alice, and Deborah Britzman. 2003. "Speculations on Qualities of Difficult Knowledge in Teaching and Learning: An Experiment in Psychoanalytic Research." *Qualitative Studies in Education* 16 (6): 755–776. https://doi.org/10.1080/0951839030001632135.

Rosen, Jonathan. 2023. *The Best Minds: A Story of Friendship, Madness, and the Tragedy of Good Intentions.* New York: Penguin.

Sacks, Oliver. 1990. *Awakenings.* New York: Vintage Books.

Sacks, Oliver. 2016. *On the Move: A Life.* New York: Vintage Books.

Swartz, Sally. 2019. *Ruthless Winnicott: The Role of Ruthlessness in Psychoanalysis and Political Protest.* New York: Routledge.

Taylor, Barbara. 2015. *The Last Asylum: A Memoir of Madness in Our Times.* Chicago: University of Chicago Press.

Togashi, Koichi. 2020. *The Psychoanalytic Zero: A Decolonizing Study of Therapeutic Dialogues.* New York: Routledge.

Waller, Willard. 2014. *The Sociology of Teaching.* Mansfield Centre, CT: Martino. First published in 1932.

Winnicott, D. W. 2014. *Through Pediatrics to Psychoanalysis: Collected Papers.* New York: Routledge. First published in 1958.

Index

www.ingramcontent.com/pod-product-compliance
Lightning Source LLC
Chambersburg PA
CBHW031305250726
48656CB00005B/1646